THE MARL HOLE KID

by

Anthony McCandless

For Lyndsey

One of the greatest gifts of being human is the ability to tell one's story. What would the world be like if all of nature could do this?

Elise McCandless

Sharing My Story

Over the past 30 years, in quiet moments, I have shared childhood stories with my wife, and when she suggested I write them down, the idea was inconceivable to me. Even though the memories sometimes seeped to the surface, I avoided focusing on them, as they always took me to a dark place.

While I was unable to work for two years during a series of back surgeries, my wife finally badgered me into writing.

We started with the Cider Bottle story. It was awful remembering that night and even more difficult trying to put it into words. At first I didn't want to show my stammer in the dialog. But strangely, I found myself stammering while telling the story.

The whole process began as sheer misery. I would get stubborn over wording and details and find myself feeling so much pain and frustration with the process that I would have to leave the room and sometimes not go back to writing for days.

I relived much of what I wrote about in nightmares and found myself awash with memories I had pushed out of my mind decades ago. When I was ready to give up, friends and family encouraged me to keep going. I couldn't see why my story would matter to anyone. What use was all of this? "Your story has always inspired me," my wife said. And so we sat and wrote, scene by scene, many of the experiences that shaped the rest of my life and who I am today.

As the months went by, I began to feel a sense of relief that these memories were outside of me—on the page. As the story progressed, the trajectory of my childhood began to take shape and everything started to make sense. Anger and resentment towards others were replaced with compassion and empathy for my younger self. I found myself able to laugh at much of the irony. For the first time in my life, I was looking at it from the outside in. I felt a strange sense of both detachment and ownership—of it all, the good and the bad. I was finally starting to heal.

In deciding to publish this book, I was inspired by the words of a friend and writing mentor: "Such stories show us that dreadful things can be survived, that painful incidents can be overcome and outgrown, and that sharing them with other human beings is an act of love."

ACKNOWLEDGEMENTS

I am forever grateful to my wife, Elise, for encouraging me to write my story and sitting down with me for the many hours and months it took to gather my thoughts and put them on paper.

My deepest gratitude to Carolyn Woolston and Liz Chapman for their generous efforts in providing feedback, editing, and support.

In addition, I'd like to thank the following individuals for their input and encouragement: Lorene Hall, Karen Moreno, Joseph Van Campen, James Van Campen, and Linda Kesler.

I did not realize how difficult this process would be, and could not have done it without the support and encouragement of all of these individuals.

Whistling Irishman

It's late Friday night and I'm sitting downstairs with my brothers, keeping warm by the fire. The bright red coals in our iron range cast a warm glow in the room. My mother is hanging nappies to dry on the metal safety bow around the fireplace. Her long, dark hair sways gently at her waist as she moves. Baby David is sleeping in his cot next to us, and Butch, our mongrel fox terrier, is snoozing on the hearth.

The warmth of the fire is making me sleepy when a familiar whistling pierces the air. Butch jumps up and dashes into the bogey hole under the stairs and I hurry to the front window to see my father swaggering toward the house. "Dad's here."

"You three had better get to bed," Mom says anxiously.

"Why?" I ask.

"I've got to have a few words with your dad."

My older brother, Leslie, and younger brother, Johnny, and I head up the bare wooden stairs to our bedroom. We climb into the double bed the three of us share.

The back door shuts and I hear my parents' voices as they move into the front room. Their conversation quickly escalates into shouting. I slip out of bed and sit quietly on the stairs in the dark, listening. I wonder why they are so angry. I hear my mother yelling and a lot of commotion and I make my way silently back down the stairs.

I open the door to the front room just in time to see my dad punch my mother in the mouth. She flies backwards over the sofa and crashes onto the metal bow of the fireplace, knocking the cot down and spilling baby David out.

Without thinking, I jump on the sofa and pounce on my dad's back. "When I'm big enough, I'm gonna do that to you!" He reaches over his shoulder, grabs me, and throws me across the room. I hit the arm of the sofa, bounce off, catch my breath, and run at him again. He knocks me down with a backhander, picks me up, and shakes me. My feet are dangling. I hear him gnashing his teeth, and I smell the booze on his breath. I swing punches at him, but my arms cannot reach his head.

"Get to bed you little idjit, before I throw you out the window!" he snarls over the din of the screaming baby.

The neighbors can hear everything through the shared wall of our houses, but no one comes to help. And we don't have a phone to call the police.

"Just leave her alone!" I shout over the ringing in my ears.

"Put him down, you drunken Irish bastard!" my mother yells as she picks up and comforts David. Still seething, my dad tosses me like a rag doll onto the armchair and stomps into the kitchen growling.

Mom grabs one of the cloth nappies littering the floor and holds it to her bleeding mouth. "You'd best get to bed while you're safe and in one piece. Go on. Now!" she urges. "Before he comes back." I don't want to leave her, but I know she's right.

I still hear them ranting as I climb into bed with my brothers, who have hidden their heads under the blankets. "What's going on?" Leslie asks nervously.

"Mom and Dad's fighting. Best just go to sleep," I say, rubbing the knot on the side of my head. I stare up at the bare lightbulb hanging from the cracked, plaster ceiling, listening to the old man roaring downstairs and wishing with all my five-year old might that I were big enough to stop him.

My England

For many people, the word "England" conjures up visions of royalty, castles, high tea, cricket, and every manner of aristocratic delight. Green, rolling hills dotted with sheep and lined with majestic oaks, quaint, thatched cottages, and picturesque farmhouses.

But in the England of my childhood, in the area known as the Black Country, men with blackened faces walk home after working long shifts, six or seven days a week. Foundries and factories spew their ashen smoke and windowsills blacken within hours of being cleaned. Some days, the smog is so thick, school children have to be led home by the hand, covering their mouths with handkerchiefs that are black by the time they get there. All around hangs the smell of soot, decades-old soot that settles in every nook and cranny, in every lung and hair follicle, on the birds and their nests, blanketing the place and its inhabitants with a stale, metallic cloud that seems to hold them there.

Many of the people who live here never leave, except to fight in a war. The place is as hard and unforgiving as the brick walls that encompass the terraced houses, the factories, and the miles and miles of canals slicing through it. Here my parents raised 13 children. I am their second son.

How It All Began

My dad, Norman Leslie McCandless, Les, was born in Coleraine, Northern Ireland, the oldest of six children in a Protestant family. In 1952, at age 21, he and his brother, Ronnie, traveled to Tipton, England, a small industrial town outside Birmingham, to find work. Les landed a job as a laborer at an iron foundry that produced engine blocks. At six feet and a muscular 200 pounds, he found the work easy. My father worked his way up to a position on the large, cupola blast furnace, so he could get regular overtime. It was dirty, hot, and dangerous work, but well paid.

Les met my mother, Joyce Herdman, in the shop on the high street where she worked. She was a tiny woman with a thick mane of long, straight, dark hair framing her delicate face and deep blue eyes. Though my mother was small, what she lacked in height she made up for in spirit. She was the second of six children, raised in a terraced council house in Tipton, squeezed between the gasworks and an iron foundry, backing up to a busy industrial canal.

Joyce's father, Bill, was a humorless man with rigid, Victorian ideas. He was tall and gaunt and walked with a cane due to World War II injuries, which prevented him from working. Because the family had to get by on Bill's meager social security income, Joyce and her siblings began working in their mid-teens.

In addition to having the responsibility of raising five girls, Bill resented the fact that his youngest child was a little slow. The boy was short and looked a lot like his mother and nothing like his father. Consequently, Joyce's father insisted till the day he died that little Bill was not his.

When Joyce introduced her father to Les, Bill told Les that if he wanted to see Joyce, he would have to meet her at the pub. When Les arrived at the pub, Joyce's father was sitting next to her. "I hear you have a job," Bill said pushing his empty beer glass forward. "It's your round."

"I don't drink, but I'll get you one," Les replied.

"If you're sitting at my table, you do now. I'll have a pint and Joyce will have a half."

With love on his mind, my father forced down his first pints of the local brew with his future father-in-law. After an hour of treating Bill to pints and trying to keep up with him, Les excused himself, went out back, and barfed it all up.

Between dates at the pub with Joyce and her father and lunchtime beer breaks with his fellow furnace men, my father's life in England began to revolve around the pub and the pint.

The Marl Hole

We live in the last house on Powis Avenue, right next to the marl hole. The street dead ends in an eight-foot, solid brick wall, with a pair of heavy wooden gates. The marl hole was created through excavating marl clay for brick making during the 1800's. When the clay mining ended in the early 1900's, the owners turned the site into a landfill. By the time we move in, the official landfill operation has ceased, and the remaining hole is about the size of a football stadium, 100 feet deep with a 50-foot-deep pool of water at the bottom. The north and south sides drop almost vertically down to the water.

Our house backs right up to the edge of the south side of the marl hole, separated from it by a six-foot spiked, metal fence. The less-steep west bank is higher than the surrounding houses and made of dirt, ash, and clay left over from the mining operations. The east bank is where trucks and tractors dumped soil and rubbish in an attempt to fill the hole before the housing estate was put in. It is the least steep of the four banks, overrun with colonies of rats and mice and haphazardly patrolled by a clan of feral cats.

Our three-bedroom, one-bath rented council house is on one end of four terraced houses. We share a wall with the Smiths, and they have to go through our back yard to get to theirs. Mr. and Mrs. Smith, who are older than my parents, have three girls and four boys; the oldest one, Alfie, is in his late teens. David (Smithy), the second youngest, is my age. He has a tuft of straw-colored hair, grey-blue eyes, and a nose

13

like Elvis Presley. Together, we are fearless and game for anything. When we're not running around getting into mischief, we're in the front yard playing marbles.

Pudding 'n Custard

Today is my first day of school. Yesterday, Mom came home with a new set of top dentures. They look shiny and white and even. After many embarrassing weeks of managing with missing front teeth, it is good to see her show her pretty smile again, though she seems to be having a little trouble eating.

Leslie, Johnny, and I are at the kitchen table having tea with hot buttered toast that Mom sliced thick off a crusty loaf. "Eat your fill, 'cause you're going to school with Leslie today." Johnny, looks up at me through his mop of golden, corkscrew curls.

"Am I going, too?"

"You can come with us, but you can't stay. You're not old enough," Mom says. "Leslie, Tony, here's a threepenny bit each for your biscuit money. Put it in your pocket. Don't lose it; I haven't got any more," she adds, snapping her purse shut. "You'll be getting a free school dinner with pudding, too." I slip the biscuit money in my trouser pocket, looking forward to milk and biscuits at break and lunch with pudding! Leslie has already told me about the apple pie and treacle pudding dripping with hot custard, with seconds if you want.

With Johnny and David both in the pram, we walk the mile to school in the crisp, September air. Highfield Road

School is a one-story brick building with a six-foot wrought iron fence around it. The school backs up to Jubilee Park. Across the street is a steep canal bank where you can see horses pulling 40-foot-long steel barges loaded with coal.

Through the gate I spy an asphalt playground surrounded by a generous L-shaped lawn. We pass through the big, iron gates and a set of double doors into an area lined with numbered hooks where the kids hang their coats. "Tarah, Mom!" Les shouts as he runs to catch up with his mates who are lining up for class. Lots of new kids are saying goodbye to their mothers; some are excited, others are crying and wanting to go home. I'm just looking forward to my hot dinner.

"Come with me, Tone," Mom says taking Johnny carefully out of the pram, so as not to wake baby David. Leaving the pram with David in the hallway, she leads us to my classroom and stands me in front of a cheerful, silver-haired lady. "This is your new teacher, Mrs. Worrell."

"Very nice to meet you, Tony," she says, resting her hand on my shoulder. "When you've said goodbye to your mother, come and meet your classmates."

"I'll pick you up at three o'clock. Now, be good." Mom smiles.

"Can I stay for pudding, too?" Johnny asks.

"No, no. We have to go home," she says, heading for the door. Johnny's big, cornflower-blue eyes sadden as he realizes he won't be getting pudding and I won't be home to play with him.

Family Fun

It's three o'clock and Mom is waiting for us outside the school gates with Johnny and David. My belly is bursting with milk, biscuits, roast beef dinner, and two helpings of apple crumble with lashings of hot custard. "Well, how do you like school?" she asks.

"I like the food," I say grinning.

Leslie laughs. "He went round twice for seconds."

Johnny gazes sadly out of the pram. He's had a lonely day.

On our way home, we notice women coming down the canal bank with buckets of coal. "Where'd you get that coal?" Mom asks a middle-aged woman with a dusty scarf tied around her head.

"Luv, the city's digging up the canal bank, exposing the coal. It's free! The workers said we can have it." She smiles, revealing a missing tooth. "I'd come back and get some while it's going."

Mom glances over at the prospectors hurrying toward the canal bank from the terraced council houses. We rush home. She empties the pram, lines it with old newspaper, and gets the shovel and bucket out of the coal place. "We'll wait for your dad to get back and you can show him where the coal is," she says excitedly, grabbing some spuds out of the pantry. "I'll stay here and make dinner."

A while later my dad gets home from work. He peels off his jacket, exposing a sweat-stained shirt freckled with small burn holes. "Les, the city workers are digging up the canal bank and there's free coal! We need to go get some while we can!"

"What do you mean free coal?" he says, taking off his shirt. His back, shoulders, and arms are speckled with spark burns that don't seem to bother him. He reaches for the bar of carbolic soap Mom uses for scrubbing clothes and has a wash in the kitchen sink.

"I just told you. They're digging it up. People are picking it and they've been told they can have it!"

"Have you no shame?" he snaps. "You want me to go picking coal like a poorhouse beggar? No way. I've just got home and I want me tay!" He puts his shirt back on, flops into a kitchen chair, and leans down to take off his heavy, scorched work boots.

"Get your own bloody tay and watch the babby! Ten shillings a hundredweight and you won't go get it for free?" Mom snaps. "Me and Tony'll go!" She pulls on an old coat while my dad snarls threats about what will happen if she doesn't get him his dinner. Fortunately, he's not drunk.

Seeing that the old man is ready to blow, Leslie decides to join us. We march out the door and make our way to the coal bank with the bucket and shovel in the pram.

We approach the canal bank and see people digging through the dirt with shovels and bare hands. "Here, missus, come dig over here. There's plenty coal for everybody!" a man in grubby overalls calls enthusiastically.

Our faces and hands blacken as we scavenge chunks of coal out of the dirt, some as large as bricks. Leslie and I take turns carrying the loaded bucket down the steep canal bank to the pram. We fill the pram with as much coal as we dare. The wheels squeak as we push it home.

"You two look like Al Jolson," Mom grins, her new teeth shining through the layer of black coal dust on her face.

"Who's Al Jolson?"

"Never mind." She smiles.

Fobbers

It's Sunday night, bath night. The cast iron range heats the water, making the living room warm and cozy. "Tony, get in the bath, it's your turn. Johnny's already in," Mom announces.

I have both hands full of marbles that I won playing Smithy this afternoon and I'm looking for somewhere to put them, so that my brothers don't nab them while I'm in the bath. I'm thinking I could slip them in one of my dad's shoes and bring it in the bathroom with me.

"Get in!" Mom urges. "The water's getting cold." I'm still rushing around the living room in underpants and a vest looking for his shoes.

"Put them marbles down and get in the bloody bath!" she shouts, exasperated. My dad jumps up from the couch and starts toward me.

"Do as your mother says," he barks. "Put the marbles down and get in the bath!"

I see him moving toward me and I stammer loudly, "I-I wa-want to." The next thing I know I'm flying across the room upside down and my left ear is ringing. Marbles are bouncing everywhere and my brothers are snatching them up like squirrels gathering nuts. The room spins around me and I catch glimpses of my brothers grabbing the fobbers. *Damn it!* As soon as I hit the floor, my dad drags me up and slaps me all around the living room.

"Leave him alone!" Mom yells. "Now what's he done?"

"He'll do as he's told! He gave me backchat!" he rants, still thrashing me.

As he chases me up the wooden stairs, my mother shouts, "He said he wanted to, you crazy Irish bastard! He's done nothing!"

While my father is momentarily distracted, I scamper to the sanctuary of my bedroom, leaving my parents arguing at the bottom of the stairs. The ringing in my ears intensifies when I pull the covers over my head.

After a while, Mom comes in. "Are you okay?"

"Yes, but get my marbles, especially my fobbers. I saw Johnny and David grabbing 'em."

"Never mind your marbles. Come downstairs. Bonanza is on. I know you like Bonanza."

"No, I'll stay here. Turn the light off." I'm thinking it's a good idea to call it a night and I'm really wishing I'd let Smithy keep his marbles.

My mom goes back downstairs and continues yelling at my dad. "Now he won't come down, you maniac. And he needs a bath!"

I hear heavy footsteps marching up the stairs. *Here we go.* My dad storms in and turns the light back on. He yanks the blankets off me and says, "I thought you said you didn't want to put the marbles down. I thought you was giving me some lip. Do you understand?"

I look up at him. "I understand."

"So, come on down. Bonanza's on."

"No thanks, I'll stay here," I say, preparing myself for round two. But Dad gnashes his teeth, turns the light off, and goes back downstairs. I hear them at it again, to the Bonanza theme song, as I get up and shut the door. I lie in the dark watching the yellow light from the gas street lamp illuminate patterns in the cracked, plaster ceiling and imagine Little Joe racing across the prairie on his paint horse. I wonder if Ben Cartwright would hire me as a ranch hand.

I'm still awake when Bonanza is over and Johnny comes to bed. "Here, I put your marbles in your sock," he says handing them to me and climbing under the covers. "Are you okay?"

I see the concern in his eyes. "I am now, thanks."

Marl Hole Visitor

The next afternoon I'm playing outside with Smithy when a giant, black beetle flies around us in circles. Smithy knocks it down with his sweater. We peek at it and marvel at its massive size. We think it must be someone's lost, exotic pet. Smithy runs and gets some fishing line and we attach it to the beetle. The mammoth insect takes off and begins flying in circles on its tether, which we find hilarious.

Out of the corner of my eye, I see my father standing in his black suit, waving me over. "Come here, I want to talk to you."

"Here Smithy, hang onto the beetle." I hand him the line and walk over to my dad.

"Come over home and get your coat. I'm taking you to Dudley Zoo. I know you like the zoo," he says without smiling.

I look him in the eye, trying to figure out what's going on. "Who else is going?"

"Just us. Come on, we've got to catch the next bus."

"No, thanks." I'm still looking him in the eye.

His gaze hardens. "What do you mean no, thanks? No backchat! Come on, let's go."

"You're only trying to make up for yesterday when you walloped me for nothing. Take Leslie and Johnny, they'd like to go." He has a wild look in his eyes, and I'm grateful he is sober. Clenching his teeth, he resists his natural urge to wallop me, turns, and marches back to the house.

I walk over to Smithy, who is still playing with the beetle. "What did he want? Do you have to go in?"

"No, it's okay, I can stay." We watch the beetle slow down in its futile attempt to get away. It lands for a moment and Smithy picks it up.

"Do you want to hold him?"

"No, let him go. Maybe he'll find his way home." Smithy cuts the fishing line and I watch the beetle enviously as it flies away from the marl hole.

Big Brother

That night Mom and Dad are arguing as I climb into bed next to Leslie, who has been listening quietly. "Leslie, why don't you help when Dad slaps Mom around?"

"What chance do we have against him? You're getting slapped around, too," he whispers in an agitated tone.

"But if you was down there with me, maybe Mom wouldn't get so hurt."

"It's not all Dad's fault. If you listen, Mom's the one who starts most of the arguments. They're as bad as one another. Just stay out of it!" He turns and pulls the covers over his head.

I stare up at the ceiling, listening and hoping they calm down for the night.

The Gift

It's the last day of school and Mom says I will be going to a new school next year for third grade because Leslie has to transfer and I have to go with him. My teachers, Mrs. Worrell and Mrs. Brown, are disappointed. "We understand your mother can't have you and your brother at two different schools, but we're sorry to see you go so soon. It was a pleasure to teach you and we're going to miss all of your lovely artwork." Mrs. Worrell smiles through sad eyes. "I'm sure you'll do well at your new school, too. We have something for you." She hands me a wrapped parcel. This is the first time anyone has given me a present like this.

"Thank you very much." I beam. I open the package and find a grey, wool balaclava. My dad tells me my head is too big for my body and, for an awkward moment, I wonder if the hat will fit.

"Try it on; I knitted it myself." Mrs. Worrell grins. We are all relieved when it fits perfectly and covers my neck down to my shoulders. For a moment I picture Mrs. Worrell sitting at home knitting the hat and maybe thinking of me.

"Come back and see us," they say, hugging me. I leave the hat on and walk home, feeling sad that this will probably be the last time I see them.

Red Butcher

It's a sunny, summer Saturday afternoon and Smithy and I are down at Bailey's Lane canal at the foot of the coal-burning power plant. The warm water from the cooling towers gets released back into the canal here and it's a good spot for coarse fishing. Every 20 feet there is a fisherman sitting on his basket and we watch as they catch fish and throw them into the keep nets for weighing. One man pulls out a large, green fish and we walk over to investigate.

"What kind of fish is that?" I ask. "It's got a big mouth."

"That there is the winner, biggest fish. That's a tench! I got him off the bottom." The fisherman grins through his scruffy beard. He removes the hook from its mouth, holding the fish carefully with his fingers in the gills. He pulls his keep net out of the water; it is thrashing with all different types of fish: shiny silver roach, striped perch, and little, whiskered gudgeon.

"You've got a lot of fish!" I exclaim.

"Ah, I pulled a good spot for the competition." He places the tench in the net and drops it back into the canal. Smithy and I can hardly contain ourselves.

"What are you using for bait?" I ask.

"Pink maggots are doing the trick today," he says pulling the top off his quart-sized bait tub. We peer in and see hundreds of squirming, bright pink maggots. He reaches in his basket, pulls out an empty Golden Syrup can, puts a few bits of bread from his sandwich in it, and hands it to me. "Throw some crumbs in to the sticklebacks and see if you can catch me a red butcher. They're the bigger sticklebacks with a bright red belly and they make good live bait. Maybe I can get me a jack pike. Now move over there and be quiet. No running up and down the bank. There's a contest on."

We lean quietly over the edge of the canal, dropping breadcrumbs that float on the surface. Little sticklebacks devour them like piranhas. We scoop up some fish but no red butcher. So we dump them back. Enthralled, we are both lying on our bellies on the tow path, hanging over the water. We pass the can back and forth, taking turns sprinkling breadcrumbs and catching fish.

"Hey, Smithy, give me the can. I can see one," I whisper, eyeing the bright red prize right in front of me. "He's a boster!" The butcher goes for the biggest crumb and starts swimming away from the bank. I push the can in the water behind him but overreach and feel myself start to slide.

"Smithy, grab my legs!" I reach back to stop myself, but slip like a crocodile into the murky water, and then surface thrashing around in the middle of the canal.

"Hey, kid, stop messing around!" a fisherman scolds. "We're trying to fish here. Swim to the side." I can hear him and I can see him looking at me but I'm unable to answer before I go under again. My feet are kicking up the black muck off the bottom and my mouth is full of foul-tasting silt and canal water.

"He can't swim!" Smithy yells.

When I surface again, the fisherman is standing up, reaching his fishing rod out to me. "Grab that, kid, I'll pull you in." I grasp the end of the pole, but when he tries to pull me, the three-piece rod separates, letting me go under again. I push off the bottom toward the clouded light above me and manage to surface once more. Through the splashing water, I see the fisherman taking his coat off.

The next thing I know, I'm lying on my side on the canal bank, coughing up muddy, brown water.

"You're going to be okay, kid," the fisherman reassures me. I can only see the outline of his face while my eyes adjust to the bright sunlight. When he comes into focus, I see that it's my neighbor Roger Grice. He stands me up and makes sure I'm breathing all right. My clothes and shoes are soaked with stinking canal water and mud. I ask him not to tell my dad what happened. He grins and pats me on the back. "Ok, I won't tell him, but you need to learn to swim, kid."

Dad's Treat

It's Saturday morning and Leslie, Johnny, and I are on the bus with my dad heading to the annual Stourport Summer Fair. The trip is 20 miles each way and we have to catch three buses to get there.

After a couple of hours, we're on the third bus and have passed through Kidderminster. The landscape transforms from factories and terraced, brick houses to sunlit, green fields and country homes. Dad is sitting happily in his black suit and white shirt, telling us about the fun fair rides overlooking the River Severn. We're all getting excited and I'm wishing I could have brought my fishing rod.

The bus drops us off near the bridge and Dad walks us over to the fair. "Can we go on the bumper cars?" Johnny asks, bouncing up and down.

"Come on," Dad says. "Let's try our luck with the coconut toss and darts!" We follow him to the booths. He wins a coconut and gives it to Leslie. Then he hits three cards with the darts and wins a golliwog and a bag of popcorn. He gives Johnny the golliwog and hands me the popcorn. "Share this with your brothers." He slips Leslie a handful of coins. "Go get yourself hotdogs and try the hoop toss. I'm just going over here to see a bloke in the pub. I'll be right back."

Hours later, the popcorn and hotdogs are long gone and we spent the last pennies on a bottle of pop to share. There is nothing more boring than being at a fun fair with empty pockets. I walk across the road to the pub, look in the window, and see my father at the bar drinking and laughing with some blokes. I head back and find my brothers sitting on a grassy bank. "What's he doing?" Leslie asks.

"He's drinking beer at the bar."

"Go tell him we need some more money."

"You go tell him, you're the oldest!"

Leslie thinks better of it and we all go down to the river looking for a big rock to break the coconut. After opening the coconut, we spot some men fishing. "Any luck?" I ask, chewing on a piece of coconut.

"Yeah, got some small fry, nothing decent yet," a weathered old man replies, sucking on his Woodbine cigarette. "Hoping to get some eels for dinner. What are you boys doing down here?"

"W-W-We're here from Tipton," I answer. "We've come for the fair."

"Tipton, that's a long way. How'd you get here?"

"On the bus."

"Who with?"

"M-M-Me dad."

"Where's he at?"

"He's in the pub."

The old man shakes his head. "Have you eaten anything besides that coconut?"

"We had a hotdog and some popcorn a while ago."

He reaches into his fishing basket and offers us some of his cheese sandwiches. We sit next to him and wolf them down while he tells us fishing stories about giant eels.

Afterwards, Johnny, Leslie, and I walk back to the place where Dad left us and spot him coming out of the pub. "Where've you been?" he asks. His breath smells of pork pies and beer. "Have you got any of the change left I give you?"

"No, we spent what you give us ages ago," Leslie answers.

"Okay, well. All right then. It's time to go." He grabs Johnny by the hand and leads us back to the main road. "Let's go."

"Pop, the bus station's over that way," I point out.

"I know. We're going this way. It's shorter," he insists.

We pass three bus stops and it occurs to me that Dad has spent our bus fare at the pub. "Are we walking all the way home?" I ask. Leslie and Johnny slow down, look at me, and then look up at Dad.

"We're gonna walk part way and ride the rest," he growls. "Save some bus fare. Let's see how far we can go before dark."

It's been hours, the sun has set, and we are still walking along the A38 toward Brierley Hill. Johnny, who is only six, is very tired. "Can we get some chips and pop and sit down for a bit?" he asks as we pass a chippy and smell the hot, salty food.

"Yeah, a bit farther up the road there's another one." Dad tosses Johnny on his shoulders. "Let's keep going."

Johnny drops his golliwog and I pick it up. "It's ok, I'll carry him." Johnny smiles sleepily down at me and hangs onto Dad's thick, wiry hair. We've been walking for hours and the last few miles have been uphill. I wish I had more cardboard to cover the hole in my shoe, but at least it's not raining. A Bedford touring van pulls up next to us. It's my dad's mate Albert from work. He's an older man with thick-rimmed glasses and an easy smile. "Don't tell him we've been to Stourport," Dad warns. "I'll do the talking."

"Paddy, is that you? What are you doing in Dudley at ten-thirty on a Saturday night with the kids?" Little Johnny, who has been sleeping on Dad's shoulders wakes up.

"Oh, we're just heading home," my dad casually replies.

"Heading home, where from? Don't you live in Tipton?"

"We've walked back from the fair in Stourport," Johnny says, rubbing his eyes.

"What! You've walked these kids from Stourport? That's sixteen miles! Bloody hell, Paddy!" Albert shakes his head as he realizes what has probably happened. He slides the van door open. "Get in! I'm taking you home."

"No, it's all right," Dad protests. "We're good. It's out of your way."

"Paddy, these kids are beat. Get in." My brothers and I gratefully climb into the van. "What, did you lose your wallet or something?" Albert persists. "How come you didn't have bus fare home?" The grilling continues all the way home, while Dad glares at Johnny. I sit back, relax, and wonder how he's going to lie his way out of this one.

Cider Bottle

It's a snowy Sunday evening. We've had our baths and are all sitting in the front room by the fire on a sofa someone just gave us. Earlier in the day we carried our old, worn out sofa around the fence to the marl hole and dumped it. Now, my brothers and I are waiting for Bonanza to come on. The younger boys are sitting on the big arms of our "new" sofa, pretending they're riding horses.

Dad is frowning and checking the pockets of his coats and trousers. "Get off the sofa!" he barks. We jump off like fleas and he yanks the cushions off, boorishly reaching down the cracks. He comes up with an old black comb, some candy wrappers, and a few coins. He counts the coins intently and looks up. "Joyce, I need another sixpence!"

"I ain't giving the kids' school biscuit money for cider! Have some tea and toast instead."

Dad begins a second round of searching. He is snarling and gnashing his teeth. He disappears upstairs. Mom replaces the cushions and we kids sit back down. "Turn the telly on and warm it up. It's almost time for Bonanza," Mom says. I turn on our rented telly and hope there's a shilling in the meter. It's a good job my dad can't open the telly coin box. Bonanza comes on once a week and I'm looking forward to watching Hoss Cartwright sort out the bad guys. I wish Hoss lived next door so he could sort my dad out. I would like to see that.

Dad appears with a sock full of coins and hands it to me. "Take these down to the Golden Cup and get me a bottle of Bulmers Cider."

"He's too young to get your bloody cider!" my mother protests. "And he ain't going out in this weather! Go yourself!"

"He can stand outside and ask somebody to get it for him."

"You're just too proud to go down to the pub and pay in small change," Mom chides.

I pull on my shoes and think that the cardboard I put in the bottoms to cover the holes is going to get wet in the snow and I'll have to replace it before I go to school tomorrow. I grab my coat and head out the door to the familiar Bonanza theme song and the cacophony of my parents arguing.

The snow is higher than my ankles and slippery. I walk the half-mile to the pub and stand for a while at the outdoor entrance, looking for someone who might help me. "M-M-M-Mr. McGee, c-c-c-could you get a bottle of cider for my d-d-dad?"

He looks down at me. "That Irish bastard sent you out in the cold! Can't he come himself?" I slip him the sock full of coins.

"What's this?"

"It's the money."

He shakes his head as he pours the coins into his jacket pocket. Minutes later he comes out with the cider and a bar of chocolate for me.

"Th-Thank you."

"No problem. Put the sock on your hand and the chocolate in your pocket. This bottle's heavy and it's cold. Watch your step." He rubs my head and watches me walk off in the snow, probably thinking of his own two sons.

This is going to be fun, I think to myself, walking gingerly, with both arms wrapped around the bottle. The deeper snow is easier to walk in and if I slip, I might not break the bottle. The cardboard in my shoes is soggy and my socks are wet. As I turn the corner onto Powis Avenue I'm met with a barrage of snowballs. Phillip Palmer and his buddy across the street are throwing them and laughing at my predicament.

"You bastards! Quit it! I can't drop this bottle!"

"Put it down and chuck some back!" they shout, increasing their ambush.

I turn away from them, hold on tightly to the bottle, and take the rest of the snowballs on my back.

Our front path is like an ice rink. I slip and slide my way to the front door and kick it, "Open up!"

Bonanza is blaring on the telly and no one seems to hear me. I wrap the hand with the sock tightly around the bottle and stretch my other arm up to the door knocker. Just as I'm knocking, the cider bottle slips and explodes on the concrete step. My father yanks the door open. "You little idjit! Was that me bottle? I've no money for another!" His fear is confirmed by the cider fumes wafting off my trousers and the step.

My father reaches down, wallops me, drags me into the house, and slams the door. The bar of chocolate falls from my pocket and lands on the floor. "That's why you dropped me bottle!" Dad hisses. "You were more worried about yer chocolate than me cider! Where'd you get the money for that? Did you pinch it?"

The walloping continues. The room spins, time slows down, and the numbness sets in. Between blows, I wonder if Mr. McGee could ever imagine what his bar of chocolate did for me tonight.

My mom comes in behind Dad and grabs him. "Leave him alone. It's your own fault, you should have gone yourself!"

31

He pushes her off, giving her a slap for good measure, while spewing his chocolate bar theory. Then he turns back to me and wallops me a few more times. "Get to bed, you idjit!" I gladly retreat to my bedroom.

I lie in the dark, listening to my parents arguing to the background of the Bonanza theme song, wondering *Where the hell is Hoss when you need him?*

Bad Egg

I'm going to Great Bridge school now with Leslie. It's a much bigger school and has a swimming program. My new teacher, Mr. Jones, is okay, but I would rather be back with Mrs. Worrell. I get good grades but it's not always fun because I'm the new kid, wear hand-me-down clothes, and I have a stammer.

"Look at him! He's scruffy and he's got holes in his shoes," a tall lad named Lee shouts, surrounded by his cronies. Some of the girls in the playground start laughing and shouting, "Scruffy McCandless!"

Lee walks up and tries to push me backwards. I turn sideways, shove him, and he hits the ground hard. One of Lee's cronies, Alan, sucker-punches me in the face and looks surprised that I'm still standing. His hit is solid, but nothing compared to the heavyweight blows I'm accustomed to at home. I look at him quietly and smile at the prospect of fighting someone my own size.

Lee and his three mates jump me together and an almighty brawl ensues. The one thing they could not anticipate is my indifference to getting hit, especially by lightweights like them. In fact, I relish the opportunity to retaliate freely.

"McCandless, quit it!" Mr. Jones grabs me mid-swing and pulls me away by my collar. "You can't be coming here causing trouble and picking fights." I don't try to explain that they started it because I won't get the words out. He marches me to the headmaster, Mr. Knock, and explains what a troublemaker I am and how I like to fight.

A few days later we're practicing our multiplication tables and Mr. Jones is calling on different kids to recite them. "McCandless, stand up! Twelve times table." I stand up and try to speak, but can't get started because of my stammer.

"Come on, McCandless, whenever you're ready." The room echoes with giggles from the girls. My face flushes and I glare at the boys, ready to settle anything they start after class.

"Okay, tough guy doesn't know his twelve times table. Sit at the front and write down what you do know." I quickly jot it all down correctly, walk over, and throw it on his desk.

I find myself scrapping regularly as the months go by. The kids from the B class continually pick fights with us kids from the A class. These brawls are a refreshing change from the more serious one-sided thrashings I get at home.

The bell rings and school is out for the day. I'm walking toward the gates when I notice Anthony, an older, spastic kid, surrounded by Lee and his gang. They're calling him names and Anthony is screaming and crying with frustration. He swings his crutch at them, misses, and falls over. Lee grabs both his crutches and throws them out of reach. Anthony begins yelling and flailing on the ground.

"L-Leave him alone!" I shout, shoving Lee out of the way. I punch one of his cronies, and reach over and grab a crutch. Correctly deducing that I might use it on them, the group takes off running. Anthony calms down and I pull him up with his crutch in my hand.

"Dank you, dank you," he says. He reaches for my wrist as two teachers approach.

"What the hell are you doing, you bully?" one shouts. "Don't you have any compassion at all?" I stand Anthony up, place one crutch under his arm, and hand him the other, as I've done many times before on the playground.

"Get away from him, you monster!" they scold, pulling me away. I try to explain but can't get the words out.

"Are you all right?" they ask Anthony, who is desperately trying to tell them what happened.

"Nodim, nodim." He points his crutch at me and garbles, "He hepped me. He hepped me!" His speech is so distorted, they can't understand him. They think he's saying that I hit him. None of the witnesses bother to explain what really happened.

"Go on, go home, get out of here," one of the teachers hisses with disgust. "We'll deal with you tomorrow." As I leave, I glance over my shoulder at Anthony, who is looking back at me.

Anthony's and my mutual inability to communicate the truth about what happened results in the teachers and administrators at Great Bridge school labeling me "a bad egg and a bully."

I take the main road home from school and am cheered to see Mrs. Worrell at her bus stop. She's wearing a blue pillbox hat and matching purse and talking to a younger woman, but she interrupts herself when she spots me. "Oh, hello, Tony! How are you? How's school going?" She gives me a big hug. I miss her and I would like to see her more often. She must be a perfect grandmother to someone and I wish it was me.

"School's fine. It's not the same." I force a smile. "How are you?"

"Oh, I'm all right," she says, looking weary. "This is Mrs. Simpson. She's a new teacher. I was just telling her about your wonderful artwork. I still have it on the wall in my classroom. I hope you're keeping it up."

The double-decker bus arrives and we say goodbye. I stand on the sidewalk waving to her, watching the bus until it is out of sight.

Rags and Brown Paper

Granddad and Grandma McCandless are visiting from Northern Ireland. Granddad is slim and smaller in stature than my dad and carries himself with a military posture. He has polished shoes and pressed trousers, a waistcoat, and shirts with pin-on collars. He is clean-shaven, with sparkling, light blue eyes and an exceptional shock of thick, white, wavy hair, neatly combed back. He smiles a lot and loves to tell Irish stories like the legend of Finn McCool and the Giant's Causeway.

Grandma is a heavy-set, surly woman of few words, and her steely, blue eyes seem to look right into you. She is used to barking orders and getting her way. Us kids instinctively give her a wide berth.

"Les, put me a chair by the window so I can watch the grandkids outside," Grandma directs. Dad rushes over with one of the coveted dining chairs and slides it carefully under her, while my mom watches from the kitchen with pursed lips. I find this new dynamic amusing.

Mom is not happy with the situation. When my grandparents are out, Mom and Dad argue about the logistics of the visit. "Put up with it, it's just for a wee while," Dad insists.

"We don't have the room and hardly enough food for the kids!"

"Don't worry, I'll work over. I'll get the extra." Mom is not reassured.

A couple of days later, Granddad is in the front room drinking tea and I'm sitting across from him working on a picture.

"Go outside and cut some wood for the fire," Dad orders.

"He's drawing me a picture, son. I'll chop the wood," Granddad suggests.

"No, you finish your tay. He can do his picture later." I drop my pencil and do as I'm told.

"You know," Granddad says, "you should go easy on that boy. You've got him running nervous. You realize you're heavier on him than the others?"

"I need to be. He's slow and he stammers like an idjit. He doesn't respect me; the others do. I need to knock him into shape before he gets too big. Look at the size of his hands, and his head."

Granddad listens solemnly. "You know he looks a lot like you when you were a kid. You had a good head, too, and you grew into it," Granddad says, looking over at me while I stack the wood.

Later that day, I ask Granddad if he's finished reading his newspaper. "I'm done with this section. You can have it." He hands me the section and folds the rest. "Whatcha making?"

"I'm gonna make a kite. I've got the cross-sticks ready, and I've made the flour-water paste."

"Here, let me help," he says. I explain what I'm trying to do and he nimbly ties the strings and cuts the newspaper. I apply the paste and we put the kite aside to dry.

"You know," he says, "that's a nice kite, but I've got another way of making one; been doing it since I was a wee lad. Let me show you." Granddad cuts the side of thick, brown paper off a 50-pound potato bag. He folds it in half, cuts a pear shape, and snips small slots every inch up the center. Then he folds the round top and cuts more slots. He threads bamboo sticks through the slots in the shape of a cross and ties them in the middle with string.

The kite is about three feet by two feet and light as a feather compared to the one I made out of pasted newspaper. "See the difference? And no paste needed. Here's the real secret. You tie a bellyband loop on the vertical stick and attach your fly string to that."

He grabs an old pair of Grandma's nylon stockings, ties them together to make one long tail, and attaches it to the bottom of the kite with a piece of string. As a final touch, he ties a strip of white rag on the end of the stockings to give the tail some weight. "Here you are, lad. All done. Let's go outside and give it a try. Bring your ball of string." His eyes are twinkling.

We walk over to the marl hole, past Alan and his gang. "What's that piece of rubbish?" they jeer. "Is that supposed to be a kite, a bunch of rags and brown paper? We've got to watch this, lads!"

Granddad takes no notice and ties the string to the bellyband. "Here, hold the ball of string and let some out." He walks about 50 feet away from me, lifts the kite up, and lets it go. The kite instantly soars high above us, as if it were being sucked into the sky. I let out the whole hundred feet of string and the kite is still tugging for more. I howl with delight. Granddad walks back toward me, smiling. "Not bad for an ol' spud bag, eh?" he says as he passes Alan and his bunch, who stomp off in disbelief.

"It's magic, Granddad! Thanks!"

Bad Wee Bastard

It's been a few weeks since Granddad showed me how to make the kite, and Smithy and I are out playing on a Sunday night. We pass in front of the Golden Cup pub and I hear a familiar song. "Smithy, give me a leg up." He laces his fingers and I climb up for a peek over the leaded-glass windows. I'm surprised and happy to see my granddad at the piano, bashing out popular songs. He is surrounded by a crowd of men holding pints, singing and laughing. I smile to myself. *Everybody likes my granddad, including me.*

The following Friday night, Dad takes his parents out for a drink, leaving Mom at home with us kids. "It's late. Tony, get the kids to bed while I dry these nappies," Mom says.

When I come back downstairs, we hear my dad and his parents bantering as they approach the back door. "Tony, get to bed, now," Mom orders. "I've got to have a word with your dad." I slip upstairs and stand quietly on the landing, listening.

"Joyce, we're back," Dad announces. "Put the kettle on fer some tay. We've had a good time at the Wagon and Horses, a nice cuppa will finish the night well!"

"I can see you have," she chides. "You've been out all night. I thought you was coming back early. I hope you have money left; you know I need to pay Willis so I can get more groceries tomorrow. Make your own tay!" she fumes. "I'm taking the babby to bed!"

"I told you to make tay!" I hear a scuffle and my granddad shouting. "Hey, Les. Les, calm down. I'll make the tay. Let Joyce get to bed." I hear the door to the stairs slam and see my mom rushing up with the baby in her arms.

"Get to your bed and close your door," she warns. "He's getting started." She shuts her bedroom door behind her. I stay on the landing and hear the melee escalating downstairs. Granddad, Grandma, and Dad are yelling and have moved into the side yard. I open the landing window and look down to see my granddad with his fists up, trying to block Dad's blows to his head. It is not looking good for Granddad. He's getting a dose of my medicine.

"Leave him alone!" I shout from the window just as Grandma drags my father off Granddad.

She lands a good punch to Dad's head. "Sober up, yer bad wee bastard and leave yer father alone!" My grandmother pushes my father against the fence, still pounding on him with both fists. Grandma, who is a Kelly, probably has my dad by 20 pounds, and now it looks like he is getting the worst of it! I start to enjoy the spectacle.

My dad looks up at me through raised arms and growls, "Get away from that window and get to bed!"

Not wanting me to witness his walloping, he tries to move away from the fence, but Grandma pushes him back. "And that's another thing," she shouts. "Stop picking on that boy of yours. He's a good wee boy! I'm tired of watching it!"

Granddad rushes in and tries to restrain both of them, but the yelling and chaos continue. I think better of enraging my dad and reluctantly take myself to bed.

I get up early the next morning wondering what today will bring. I make my way downstairs and see my grandparents sitting at the table in the front room.

"Here, son, come and sit by yer grandma and have some tay and toast with me." She pulls out a chair, pours some tea, and hands me a large piece of crusty loaf toast slathered in butter. "Yer granddad went out early fer the paper and got the loaf and butter."

"Thanks, Granddad," I say, looking over at him.
He smiles. "No worries, lad, glad to do it. By the way, yer dad was up early with me and is off to work on his bike, so sit, relax, and enjoy your toast."

Granddad has a fat lip and a bruise over his eye, but it doesn't seem to bother him. I wonder what my dad looks like as I glance over at Grandma, who is smiling, with the mug of tea looking tiny in her hands.

Mom joins us at the table. "When you've finished your tay, Tone, I want you to go over and see Mr. Willis. We'll have bacon and eggs when you get back."

A few days after the big fight, Mom gives my dad the nickname Bunjy, after a character from a comedy television show called Me Mammi. It's about a grown Irishman whose heavy-set mother still pushes him around and tells him what to do. The nickname infuriates my dad, which suits Mom fine.

Singing Uncle George

I'm doing homework in the front room.

"Clear the table off," Bunjy barks at me. "We need to set up for dinner."

"C-C-Can I just finish this? It's for school." Leslie looks over and laughs. He finds my stammer amusing. *I'll deal with him later.*

"No, clear it off now!" Dad orders. "And stop stuttering! You sound like an idjit."

More giggles from Leslie.

Granddad eyes my father intently. "You know it's because of you that he does that." Shooing Leslie out of the room, he adds, "You're just making it worse."

Granddad sits down next to me. "Don't worry about the stammer. It's an Irish thing. My brother George had it when he was young. And he grew up to be a fine man. Take your time, and if you need to, sing the words in your head before you speak. That's what your great-uncle George did to fix it."

Dad looks surprised to learn that one of his favorite uncles stammered as a kid.

Granddad picks up my schoolwork and we move over to the sofa. He recounts how his brother George, who was over six feet tall, could hold a dozen eggs in one hand. "Someday you'll be big and strong like your great-uncles," he says, smiling gently.

Bunjy shakes his head and leaves the room. Granddad tells me more stories about our Irish family. I listen eagerly, wondering how all of this could culminate in an ogre like my dad. I realize I'm not stammering as I talk to Granddad.

A few days later, I come downstairs to find Granddad and Grandma in the front room with their bag packed. "We have to get back home to Ireland for now. But we'll be back," Granddad says, giving me a hug. I watch sadly as they leave, with Bunjy carrying their big, worn leather case to the bus stop for them. Then I walk to my spot on the grassy bank at the marl hole with Granddad's kite and sit quietly.

The Trade

It's a fine, sunny day and I'm playing in the back yard. I hear the brass bugle of a scrap man announcing his arrival and run into the street to see which one it is. It's Ben, the rag and bone man, who has trinkets to trade with us kids. He places a nosebag full of oats on his stocky, brown horse and starts opening boxes on his cart.

I look inside one of the boxes and see a few dozen peeping, little, yellow chicks. "What do I have to do to get some of those?" I ask excitedly as the neighborhood kids gather.

"Chickens for rags. Hurry up, before they all go," he announces as he opens another box filled with masks, marbles, and whistles.

I run into the house. "Mom, the rag and bone man's here!"

"I heard him. Let's see what we've got," she says, heading over to the bogey hole. Mom is not proud. People are always giving her bags of unwanted clothes. She puts old coats on our beds at night to keep us warm, and one of us will usually be able to wear some of the hand-me-down shoes or clothes. But anything we really can't use goes in the bogey hole under the stairs.

Mom gives me an armful of rags. I run to Ben and hand them over. He grabs a little cardboard box, puts four chicks in it, and gives them to me. I'm ecstatic. I only wish I could have a few more. "Wait a minute, Ben, I'll get some more rags."

I rush back to the bogey hole and find a bag with an old work coat and clothes in it. Mom is upstairs, so I grab the bag and dash back to the cart. "Here, can I get four more chicks?"

Ben opens the bag and is pleasantly surprised. "Sure, you can choose them yourself this time." As I'm picking my chicks, Ben inspects the coat. "Are you sure about this duffle coat?"

"Yes!" I say. "Can I have a bigger box and some straw?"

"'Course you can. Anything else you got for me?" he says, slipping on the coat.

I take off with my new little friends, and Ben rides off in his new coat. Nothing can dampen the joy of the moment.

All the neighborhood children flock to me to have a look at the fluffy, peeping chicks. I walk into the kitchen with a trail of kids behind me and put the box on the table.

"Chickens! What the bloody hell have you done?" Mom asks suspiciously. "Where are you going to keep them and how'd you get so many?" She walks over to the bogey hole and sees that the second bag is gone. "You didn't take the other bag, did you?"

She can tell by my face that I did. "Oh, bloody hell! Bunjy wanted that duffle coat. Go get after him and get it back!"

"He's gone," I say, hoping she won't find out that he's already wearing it.

"Oh dear, what am I gonna tell Bunjy when he gets back from work?" Mom laments. "He's gonna figure it out and beat you up and down!"

I put the box of chicks by the fireplace, thinking that whatever happens, it will be worth it if I can keep the chicks.

"What you gonna feed them little buggers?" Mom asks. "Where are you gonna keep 'em? They're gonna need a hutch."

"I'll get some scrap wood off the marl hole and build one."

Seeing how attached I already am to my little, peeping buddies, Mom relents. "Okay, then. Let's try them with some bread and milk." She makes a little bowl of food for them and they tuck into it.

Later that evening I'm sitting next to my chickens in the front room when Bunjy comes in and hangs his coat. He pulls off his leather belt, folds it in half, and cracks it loudly. "Joyce, have the kids been good?" He looks at me. "Wipe my bike down and put it away."

He notices the box and walks over. "What you got there?"

"Chicks. I got them from the rag and bone man."

"So, Ben's giving out chicks now, is he? That's good. They'll make a nice dinner when they're growed."

The bogey hole is right behind him and I'm hoping he doesn't look inside it.

"Joyce, where's me tay? I'm going to have a pint over the Wagon and Horses."

I cringe, picturing him walking into the pub and seeing Ben. "Hey Paddy!" Ben would say. "Like me coat?"

"What's wrong with your face?" Bunjy barks. "Go get me bike cleaned!" Mom walks past with a plate of food, glaring at me.

I wipe down the bike and put it in the coal place while Bunjy finishes his tea. He goes upstairs to change, and then I watch nervously as he emerges with a clean shirt on. I'm relieved when Mom finally hands him his coat and gets him out the door.

"You're lucky he didn't remember that other coat," she warns. "It's nicer than what he's wearing. It's only a matter of time until he figures it out."

It's been a few days since I got my chicks. I'm changing the newspaper in the box when I see Bunjy look in the bogey hole. "Joyce! Where's that bag with the coat in it?"

"What bag? What coat?" Mom says, looking sideways at me. I continue cleaning the box, wondering if this will be the end of my budding career as a chicken farmer.

"It was in that last load of bags you got."

The chicks peep innocently, oblivious to the precariousness of their situation.

"I sorted through that lot days ago and threw out the stuff I thought we didn't want. If there was something you needed, you should have took it out."

My heart pounds, waiting for his response.

"Well, what were you thinking? There was a coat in there I could've used! What did you do with it?"

"I threw the stuff I didn't want over the marl hole. I need the room in the bogey hole for the washing."

Bunjy snarls at her and marches out the kitchen door. I follow him, hoping he isn't going over to the marl hole to look for the bag. I'm relieved to see him smoking in the back yard. Mom is watching him over my shoulder. "Close the box and keep them chickens quiet," she says. "It looks like he hasn't figured it out yet."

Mrs. Worrell

It's Monday afternoon and I'm heading home alone from school. I decide to go along the main road, hoping to see Mrs. Worrell. Mrs. Simpson is standing in line at the bus stop and watches me approach. She lowers her head. I look around. "Where's Mrs. Worrell? Did she not work today?"

She puts her hand gently on my shoulder, pulling me aside. "Mrs. Worrell won't be catching the bus anymore, Tony. She's moved on."

"Moved on where?"

"She passed away last week at home, peacefully," she says with tears in her eyes. "We will all miss her very much."

Not sure what to say or do, I look up at Mrs. Simpson. She is still talking, but I no longer hear her words. *Why is it everything I care about goes away?* Dazed, I turn and make my way home.

"Where's my balaclava, Mom?" I ask as I walk in the kitchen.

"It's in the sideboard drawer with the socks, but surely you won't be needing that today."

I stuff the balaclava in my pocket, head over the marl hole to my spot on the grassy bank, and sit quietly.

Knock Out

Johnny and I each have a pair of red boxing gloves. We're upstairs in Susan and Sheelagh's bedroom, setting up an "official" boxing match. We designate the double bed as the ring. There is no electric light fixture in the room, only a drop-cord bulb holder clamped on the picture rail, which is plugged into the light socket in the hallway. I have the bright idea to take the bulb out and use the holder as an announcer's microphone. I check the switch in the hallway to make sure it is off and remove the bulb.

"And now, it's round one of the world champion boxing match!" I clamp my "microphone" back onto the picture rail and we have a few rounds. "Here we are in round three of the championship match. And Johnny the Slugger is lagging behind Tony Hammerhand." I hold the mike right up to my mouth, just like a real sports announcer. At that moment my sister Sheelagh flicks the hall lightswitch on, and my lights go out.

"Mom, the hall light's not working."

I wake up and Johnny is standing over me with his boxing gloves still on. "That was a good 'un!" I say, "But you've gotta wait 'til I put the mike down!"

"I didn't hit you. It was the bulb holder. You just sort of jumped and lay on your back with your eyes closed. You've been lying there a couple of minutes."

Over Johnny's shoulder I see Bunjy standing in the doorway, checking out why the hall light is broken. "Where's the bulb to the light?"

48

"It's over here," Johnny explains. "Tony took it out to use the bulb holder as a mike and it knocked him out."

"What do you mean it knocked him out?"

"He put it up to his mouth and it knocked him out." They both look at me lying on the bed, still drowsy.

"You idjit!" Bunjy barks, peppering me with slaps to the head. Johnny jumps out of the ring and runs downstairs. He doesn't want any part of round four with the crazy Irishman. The blows gradually bring me back to my senses, and I'm relieved by the sound of my mother's voice calling off the match. Bunjy marches back downstairs, mumbling about his idiot son.

I lie on the bed with my red boxing gloves still on, thinking of the day I will have this match with Bunjy when I'm a heavyweight, too.

Monty

The chickens are about seven months old. My favorite is a feisty, golden rooster I named Monty. He comes when I call him and lets me pick him up. At dawn, he and a rooster up the street take turns crowing.

It's Saturday afternoon and I have Monty in my arms when I turn around and see Bunjy back from the pub, stinking of beer and eyeing my rooster. "Is that the little bugger that wakes me up in the morning?"

I stroke Monty's head.

"Let me show you something," Bunjy says, "Give him to me."

I reluctantly hand him over and follow Bunjy into the kitchen. He opens the drop leaf table and stretches Monty along the line between the leaves, holding his head still for a few moments. "Now stay there and don't move," Bunjy commands, pointing his finger at the rooster. I'm dumbfounded to see that Monty remains perfectly still; the only thing moving is his eye, blinking and looking at me.

My brothers and sisters have gathered around. "Bloody hell!" little David exclaims. "Even the chicken does as he's told!" The younger children stare wide-eyed and gobsmacked.

Mom comes into the kitchen. "What's going on?" she asks, surveying the crowd of children.

"We're gonna have chicken for dinner," Bunjy announces. "Where's me chopper?"

I look down at Monty, hoping he did not understand that. "No, not Monty," I say, looking at my mother. As I'm

50

pleading with her, Bunjy grabs Monty by the feet and carries him outside, a flock of kids in tow. The rooster has awakened from his trance and is squawking and flapping his wings. My father holds him down on a big yellow marl clay rock in the yard.

"Watch this!" he shouts and chops Monty's head off. He quickly grabs the rooster and stands him up. I watch in horror as a headless Monty runs up the garden flapping his wings, letting out an eerie drone until he crashes into the fence and falls onto his side. I rush over and pick him up. His legs are still moving. The last bit of air wails out of his throat, and he goes limp. In disbelief, I look down at my once-animated, feathered friend.

"He crashed into the fence 'cause he couldn't see where he was going!" Bunjy cackles, looking over my shoulder.

"Give him here." Bunjy pulls poor Monty from my arms and carries him into the kitchen. I walk over to the rock and pick up Monty's head to bury it.

Bunjy calls me into the kitchen. I slip Monty's head in my pocket and go inside. I see that he has already cut Monty's feet off. "Get this chicken plucked," Bunjy orders.

"I'll do it," Mom offers.

"No, he can do it. If he wants to raise chickens, he's got to learn how to dress them." He picks up Monty. "Look, you grab it like this and pull the feathers." He yanks out a couple of handfuls and hands me my maimed, partially plucked friend.

Mom comes to help me while Bunjy chases the kids with my rooster's foot, which he is opening and closing by pulling the tendons. He has a fiendish look on his face as the children squeal and run away.

As I stand at the sink and pluck feathers, I come to the dreadful realization that Monty's family will all go the same way he did, and soon. I think of how I built the new stairs for the chicken house and found the plastic on the marl hole to

51

keep the rain out, unaware that my career as a chicken farmer would be over so quickly. When these are gone, I will never raise chickens again.

Nailed

I'm playing in the snow with my mates at the marl hole. We're tired of chucking snowballs, and wishing we had a sled. The side of the tip is steep where the trucks dump their loads. We try sliding down the bank on our arses and end up getting soaked. The old socks I'm using for gloves are sopping wet, too.

My mate Phillip grabs a discarded plastic kitchen dish pan and tumbles down the hill with his arse wedged into it. We all laugh. "What?" he says indignantly. "Me arse is frozen. I need something to slide on!"

Smithy grabs an old, plastic fertilizer bag and climbs inside. "Give me a push!" He makes it about halfway down and finishes up in a heap.

Suddenly, I remember an old, enamel gas cooker that I had tried to scavenge a burner from for our cooker at home. I run over and see that the detachable part of the top is still there and drag it up the bank.

"Where you gonna sit with all them burner holes?" my mates ask.

"I'm gonna put my arse right here over the pilot hole in the middle, and I'm gonna hang onto the sides. Give me a push!"

I slide perfectly down the bank and bring the stovetop back up for my friends to try. We take turns and eventually make a nice sled run.

"Right, give me a good hard push," I say. "I want to make it to the bottom this time." Smithy and Phil give me a mighty shove and I go zooming down the bank and catch air off the mound at the bottom. The stovetop and I part ways in flight and I land on top of a snowy heap of junk. My mates come running over.

"Whoa, that was the best yet!" Smithy shouts. "Have another go!"

"No, I'm done, I'm going home. Beat that!" I say, feeling winded.

I get home, go in the bathroom, peel off my frozen pants, and sit down with my Dandy comic. After a few chuckles at Desperate Dan the cowboy sheriff, I tear off a piece of newspaper to wipe. As I reach back I feel something sticking out of the right cheek of my arse. It feels like a large nail head.

I hear my mother on the other side of the wall in the kitchen. "Hey, Mom, come in here. I think I've got a nail stuck in my arse!"

"What do you mean you've got a nail in your arse?"

"Come and have a look!"

I pull the chain to flush and my mother comes in. "Where?" I point to it, unable to see it myself. She bends down for a closer look, grabs the head of the nail, and tries to pull it out. "It doesn't budge. Johnny walks in for a look. "Go get your Dad," Mom tells him.

Johnny goes to the fireplace and I hear him say, "Mom wants you. Tony's got a nail in his arse."

"What?" Bunjy marches into the bathroom to find me across my mother's lap as she tries to pull the nail out. "Now what you done, you idjit!" he snaps, reaching for the nail. I

53

feel myself lifted off of my mother's lap and now I'm dangling by the nail in my arse.

"There's no room in here. Let's take him in the front room on the sofa," Bunjy orders, carrying me out of the crowded bathroom.

"Get me trousers!" I plead while my sisters look on, giggling.

"Never mind your bloody trousers," Bunjy shouts, laying me across his lap. The only thing clenching harder than my dad's teeth at that moment is my right arse cheek. "Keep still and relax!" Bunjy barks and wallops me.

"Stop hitting him! He can't help it!" Mom shouts. I marvel at my dad's ability to simultaneously hold me down, yank a nail out of my arse, and slap me.

"This bloody thing won't come out! I need some pliers to get hold of it. Go ask Alf next door if he can lend me a pair. Don't tell him what it's for; he won't believe it."

I'm lying on Bunjy's lap wondering how something I didn't even feel go in could be such a bastard coming out.

Johnny comes back with a pair of vice grips and hands them to Bunjy. With an audience of snickering siblings, Leslie, Johnny, and Mom hold me down as Bunjy clamps onto the nail and tugs, slowly dragging it out. He grimaces. "Even his arse is stubborn!"

Bunjy inspects the rusty nail in the vice grips and then glances over at me. "How did you manage to get a six-inch nail in your arse and not know it, you idjit?"

I try to explain, but my mother interrupts. "Does it matter? It's out now. He needs to get a tetanus shot," Mom insists, then asks me, "Can you walk to the bus stop?"

An hour later, Bunjy drops me off at Dudley Guest Hospital emergency room. "Here, they will probably want to see that." He thrusts the six-inch nail into my hand and heads down the street for a pint.

I explain what happened to the admitting nurse, who can't help but smirk. "I'm sorry, I know it's not funny. How did you get here? Can you walk okay?" She tries to hide a smile.

"I c-came on a bus."

"Who with?"

"M-me dad."

"Where is he now?"

"I don't know." I avoid mentioning the pub.

"Okay, never mind. Let's get you taken care of."

The nurse leads me to an exam room and pulls the curtains. "Now take off your trousers and lie down." She cleans the wound and leaves to get the doctor.

Moments later, the curtain opens and three grinning young nurses step in. I'm lying on my belly with a bare arse wondering how this can get any more awkward. They look at my chart and ask me to explain what happened.

"I f-f-fell down," I say, embarrassed. Tittering, they inspect my backside and the nail.

"What, you fell onto a six-inch nail?" one of them asks. "Turn over."

"No, I'm not t-t-turning over; it didn't go through."

At that moment, the doctor comes in, eyes the nurses skeptically over his glasses, and dismisses them. I breathe a quiet sigh of relief.

After a thorough examination, he announces, "You're a lucky young man!" I watch him turn the nail over in his gloved hands and shake his head. "This could have been a lot worse. The nail missed the bones and major blood vessels." He hands me the nail. "I suppose you'll want to keep this."

After the doctor leaves, an older nurse with kind eyes comes in to give me a tetanus shot and dress the wound. She then escorts me to the waiting room, instructing me to come back in a couple of days.

After a while, Bunjy shows up, reeking of beer. "What did they say?"

"Th-th-they said that I was lucky, it could have been a lot worse."

After a long, uncomfortable bus ride home, we are greeted by my brothers, who come rushing over. "Now you've two holes in your arse," Johnny taunts. "You'll be able to fart twice as loud!" He is blissfully unaware of what is in store for him a few weeks down the road.

Health Inspection

My teacher, Mr. Jones, is writing math problems on the chalkboard. I look over to my classmate Robert and ask, "Can you see that from here? I think he needs to write bigger."

"Yeah, I can see it fine, can't you?"

"No, it's fuzzy for me." I raise my hand.

"Do you have a question, McCandless?"

"Can I sit nearer the board? I can't see so well from here." This is met with a chorus of giggles and whispers from the class.

"Yes, of course." Mr. Jones gestures to one of the seats in the front row. "This is a first. Normally I only put people who are misbehaving at the front."

A few days later, I'm at the weekly health inspection by the district nurses. This is part of the national health program that provides free milk and lunches to school kids. Mr. Jones had let us know the day before that they were coming and reminded us to wash our feet, behind our ears, and under our fingernails, and to put on fresh socks for the occasion.

A girl ahead of me goes bright red as the nurse who has been looking in her hair escorts her to a separate room. "Uh oh, Janet's got nits!" one of the boys taunts.

It's my turn and the nurse meticulously parts sections of my hair, looking for lice, then inspects my ears and mouth. She checks out my hands and feet for warts, boils, and signs of malnutrition. "Okay, everything looks good. Is there anything else you want to talk to me about?" she asks in a gentle voice.

"No, I don't think so," I answer casually. I'm hoping she doesn't ask me about my home life like she did with Stanley Lowther, a kid whose family is even poorer than mine.

She checks her chart. "Well, Mr. Jones mentioned you had trouble seeing the blackboard." She looks in my eyes with a light. "I'm going to send you to see Dr. Pike, the optometrist in Great Bridge."

It's Saturday morning and I'm at the farmers market in Great Bridge with my mom. She comes here when she has cash; otherwise she gets credit at Mr. Willis's grocery store across the marl hole.

She goes to her favorite veggie stand first. It is manned by Joe, a brawny bloke in his forties who is wearing dungarees over an old, grey sweater. "How much a pound for them King Edward spuds, Joe?"

"Threepence a pound, Joyce."

"How much for twelve pound? Give me a deal and I'll buy some cabbage."

"Give me half a crown then." Mom nods, and he weighs out the spuds. He fills a paper bag and throws in a large swede. "Here, boil that with them spuds and mash it all together; it's good." He reaches her the bag with a callused hand.

Mom continues haggling around the stands, loading bags with crisp carrots, cabbage, cauliflower, brussels sprouts, and giant Bramley apples, then hands them to me to carry.

"While we're here, we'll go see that Dr. Pike about your eyes." We walk into the shop and he takes me right away. He looks in my eyes with his light and homes in on my right eye. Then he asks me to read the chart. I'm not able to read below the second line of letters. Dr. Pike turns the lights off and further examines my eyes.

My mom pokes her head in. "What's taking so long? We have a bus to catch."

The doctor flicks the light back on. "He seems to have a lazy right eye. I'll get you an appointment with the ophthalmologist at Dudley Guest Hospital."

"Is it bad?" she asks, looking worried.

"Oh, it'll be okay. Just make sure you take him to the eye doctor, then come back and see me and we'll fix him up with some glasses." He smiles tentatively.

We thank Dr. Pike and head to the corner cafe for the market day special, a cup of tea and a thick slice of toast for sixpence. This is our treat while we wait for the bus. "We're going to need a half-day off school to go to the eye doctor." Mom sips her tea. "How do you feel about wearing glasses?"

"If I can see better at school, I don't mind."

"You might get teased a bit."

"That's okay. I can thump a few heads." I grin. "That'll stop the teasing."

A few weeks later, Mom and I are at the Dudley Guest Hospital, talking to the eye specialist, who is short with thick glasses that rest on his pink, round cheeks. He spends a long time examining my eyes. "He needs to wear glasses and should have a blank over his good eye for a few hours a day. We can set you up an appointment with Dr. Pike to make the glasses. Then you can come back and see me in a couple of months to check that your right eye has improved." He pats me on the shoulder and forces a long-toothed smile.

Bunjy has come home from work and is sitting at the table eating his pork chop with mashed spuds. I sit near him and watch, hoping he'll give me the bone to chew on since us kids only ever get fatty, belly draft pork. Mom is sitting next to him, having a cup of tea. "We went to the eye specialist today and he says Tony's got a problem with his right eye. Dr. Pike is going to set him up with a pair of glasses that will blank out his good eye."

Bunjy stops chewing. "Glasses! No kid of mine is going to wear glasses! No McCandless has ever worn glasses.

Especially blanked-out glasses. He'll look even more like an idjit!" He glares at me and throws his pork chop bone to Butch, the dog, who gnaws on it with as much delight as I would have.

The Phone Box

I'm nine years old. It's Saturday and Mom's washing nappies while Dad is at the pub. I'm helping by turning the handle on the wringer. Mom is pregnant with her seventh child and looks uncomfortable and awkward as she works. "Go hang these outside on the line and I'll put the kettle on and we'll have a cuppa," she says.

I head out with the damp nappies as she waddles into the bathroom. When I return, she's sitting at the kitchen table with two steaming cups of tea. "When we've finished these, I need you to go across the marl hole to the phone box and call the ambulance."

"What for?"

"I think the baby's about ready."

"Do you want me to go find Bunjy at the pub?"

"No. No time for that," she says calmly. "Just dial 999."

I run across the marl hole wondering how I'm going to do this. Luckily, the phone box is empty, because the next one I know of is a mile away.

I dial the number.

"Hello, emergency services. How can I help you?" I try to get the words out, but nothing comes.

"Hello? Is anyone there?"

I feel my face flush and beads of sweat on my temples. Someone walks up and waits to use the phone. I inhale sharply, but as usual my first word is stuck in my throat.

"Hello?"

"Uhhh, uhhhhh…"

"Calm down love, and tell me what you need. Fire, police, or ambulance?"

"B-BABY! BABY!" I blurt out. "Me mother is having the baby."

"Okay, ambulance, good. I can help you with that. Can you give me the name and address?"

I'm stuck again, and then I remember how Granddad told me to relax and sing the words in my head before I speak. It works. Luckily, 262 rhymes with Powis Avenue.

"Okay, love. The ambulance is on the way."

I relinquish the phone box, feeling a wave of relief followed by a sharp shot of self-loathing. I run back to the house, and I know that whatever it takes, I'm going to fix this damn stammer.

Moving Target

My dad's younger brother Roger from Northern Ireland is staying with us. He has come looking for work and a fresh start. Unlike my dad, Roger is always cheerful and friendly to us kids. He is smaller than my dad, with smiling eyes and thick, dark, wavy hair done up like Tony Curtis, which he tarts up with Brylcream on the weekends. Instead of going out drinking, Roger goes to the dances and charms the ladies.

It's Saturday afternoon and Uncle Roger is with us in a field across the street from the Horsely Tavern, letting us try his new pellet gun. Bunjy has suggested we set up here so that he can have a few pints while Roger entertains us.

Uncle Roger places empty baked beans cans on a bank about 40 feet in front of us. I'm excited. I've never shot a pellet gun before. He breaks the barrel open, licks the lead .22 pellet, and slips it in the breach. "Now make sure you don't put the pellets in upside down. Works best with the skirt up, like the ladies." He grins.

"I don't understand," I say.

"Never mind, you will when you're older." He snaps the rifle closed, shows us how to line up the sights, and then fires and knocks one of the cans down.

"That was lucky!" I say. "Do it again." He knocks another one over with ease.

"Can I have a go?" I ask.

"Yeah, of course," Roger says. "Hey Johnny, go stand them cans back up." He loads another pellet. Johnny and David are dashing around excitedly. "Okay boys, that's good.

Now get well out of the way." He hands me the gun and Johnny and David disappear over the bank.

"Lean it against your right shoulder and line up the sights with the can. Hold it steady."

"I can't see too good out of that eye. Can I try the other side?"

"Well, you're right-handed, but it should work." I move the gun to my left shoulder and take aim while Roger coaches me. "Now, hold your breath and pull the trigger nice and steady."

Just as I pull the trigger, Johnny comes dashing back over the bank, with David close behind him and runs right in front of the cans.

Crack! The gun goes off. Instead of the ping of the pellet hitting the can, we hear Johnny shriek and fall over holding his leg.

"Oh shit! You shot Johnny!" Roger shouts. He rushes over to look at Johnny's leg. The pellet has gone straight through the flesh on one side of his calf and out the other side. He has two holes about an inch and a half apart.

I walk over, still carrying the rifle. "Why did you shoot me?" Johnny whimpers, looking up at me through watery eyes.

"You run right in front of the target!"

"Am I gonna die?" Johnny groans.

"You've been watching too much Bonanza. You'll be fine." Roger ties his handkerchief around Johnny's leg.

"What's going on?" Bunjy's voice booms from a few feet away. The pub is closed for the afternoon and he stinks of beer. He glances over at me holding the rifle.

"Tony shot me in the leg while David was chasing me."

"What do you mean Tony shot you in the leg? Roger, you let that little idjit loose with that bloody rifle of yours? You know better than that. Give me that pellet gun!" Bunjy orders, yanking it out of my hands. The shoulder strap is still around my neck and that pulls me toward him. He lifts it off and wallops me around the head, knocking me to the ground.

Roger jumps in. "Wait a minute, it wasn't his fault. Johnny ran in front of the target!"

"Put that rifle back in the case!" Bunjy scolds. "What if the coppers come? What am I gonna tell them at the hospital?"

"Tell them what happened," Roger replies. "It was an accident. He's not badly hurt. Just put a plaster on it and forget about it."

"It don't work like that over here. I have enough trouble with the coppers. Now go home and tell Joyce what happened. We'll get the next bus from here"

An hour later we're at Dudley Guest Hospital with Bunjy. On the way over he has coached us not to mention the pellet gun. "If they ask you what you did, Johnny, tell them you fell on some fence wire. Got it?" We all nod our heads.

Bunjy tells the admitting nurse the fence wire story and we're called into the treatment room. "And what happened here?" the nurse asks, removing the handkerchief and reading the admission notes. "You've got two holes in your leg."

Johnny looks up at her and points at me. "My brother Tony shot me in the leg with the pellet gun."

The nurse looks over at my dad, then back at the admission notes. We all cringe.

"Take no notice of him, he's got a big imagination." Bunjy insists with a grinchy smile. "He cut his leg on some fence wire." He glares at Johnny who stares back, wide-eyed.

After Johnny's leg is bandaged, we all walk back to the bus stop. Bunjy is seething. "I told you not to mention the pellet gun!" he barks, shaking Johnny by the arm.

Johnny shrugs. "I'm sorry, but she asked me." He holds his hands up, expecting a clip on the ear, but instead I'm the lucky recipient of the thick ear.

"What is it with you?" Dad rants. "Nothing but trouble, you can't do anything right." His booze breath wafts in my face. "Och, you're useless!"

We get home, and Mom rushes out expecting to see Johnny with part of his leg blown off.

She grabs Johnny and walks him into the house. We all follow her in.

"Fancy going drinking and shooting with kids running around!" Mom scolds Bunjy. "You stink of beer!"

"It was your idjit son who shot him, not me!" Bunjy retorts.

"Oh, shut up and get out of here!" she growls like a mother bear while gently stroking Johnny's head.

"Come on, Roger. You can buy," Bunjy says as they head out the door.

Johnny Joins the Club

It's been a few weeks since I got the nail in my arse sledding down the tip. Johnny and I are upstairs in our bedroom, which has two queen beds side by side for me and my three brothers. We have our red boxing gloves on and we're setting up for a match. There's a bike leaning against the bottom of one of the beds because we don't have room for it downstairs, and Mom doesn't want to leave it outside to get stolen. It was given to us by our cousin Lynn Kelly, who got a new one. The bike rides fine, but the saddle is a little worn and has a bolt sticking out the back of it.

"And now for round one with Tony Hammerhands and Johnny the Slugger. It's a one-round match, going for a knockdown!" I announce, reaching over the footboard to ring the bell on the bike's handlebars. As I turn back around, Johnny clobbers me and knocks me down.

"The winner! The winner!" he shouts, hopping back and forth between the two beds like Tigger and holding his arms in the air.

"Wait a minute, give me a chance. I wasn't ready yet!" I protest. I reach over and ring the bell again, this time keeping my eye on him. Johnny pounces, swinging his fists and yelling. He leaps right onto my swinging fist and takes one on the chin. He flies over the footboard and bounces off the bike onto the floor with a yelp.

"It's a knockdown. The winner!" I gloat, looking over at Johnny who is getting up slowly, holding his arse.

"I hurt my arse on the bike. I think it's bleeding," he whimpers.

I jump off the bed. "Turn around, let me have a look." There's a small tear in his trousers. "I don't see any blood. Pull your trousers down."

The bolt on the saddle has torn a hole in his left arse cheek and I can see the blue muscle inside. I can hardly believe my eyes and burst out laughing. "Now you can fart twice as loud, too! See what you get for teasing me about the nail?"

Johnny stands in front of the wardrobe mirror and, at the sight of his wound, begins to howl and jump around, while I'm still cackling over the irony.

Mom bursts into the room to investigate the commotion, and shrieks when she sees Johnny's torn arse. She grabs him and shouts, "Les, you better come and see this!" I hear Bunjy coming up the stairs. Mom turns toward me. "What's so funny?" she asks.

I stop laughing and try to explain.

Bunjy barges in and looks at Johnny's open wound. "What happened?"

"We were boxing," Johnny explains. "Tony knocked me off the bed onto the bike saddle and I hurt my arse."

"You little idjit!" Bunjy snarls at me through gritted teeth. "I heard you laughing. You think this is funny?" He grabs me by the shirt and starts walloping me around the ears. I try to block him with my boxing gloves, but that only enrages him. He picks me up and throws me on the bed.

"Leave him alone! It was an accident!" Mom shouts as he continues to slap me around. "Why do you always have to go after *him*?" I try to block his blows, dismayed by the turn of events. When I set up my match with Johnny, I didn't think I'd be going from lightweight to bare knuckle heavyweight in one round.

House Rules

It's Saturday night and Bunjy's at the pub. The kids are in the front room playing and Mom is having a cup of tea. "Tony, it's getting late. Get the kids to bed," she says, checking on baby Jean in the cot. Leslie, grabs his Beano comic and heads upstairs.

"All right. Up to bed," I announce, trying to usher my younger siblings to their rooms.

"Why do we have to go to bed now?" Johnny and David complain. "How come Tony gets to stay up?"

"Never mind, just get to bed and be quiet up there," Mom insists.

A few minutes later, David and Johnny are still running around on the upstairs landing. I give them each a wallop and chase them into their bed.

David is howling with temper while rubbing his ear, when Mom appears behind me. "What's going on? What happened here?"

"Tony hit me hard!" David wails. "And why can't we wait downstairs with you 'til Dad gets home?"

Mom wallops me up the side of the head. "Bloody hammer hands!" she shouts. "Don't hit so bloody hard. Don't be like Bunjy!" She turns to my younger brothers. "Now calm down and get to sleep."

Rubbing my cheek, I watch her as I try to figure out the rules. *Dad hits Mom and all of us kids. Mom hits Dad and all of us kids. I can hit my younger siblings but not too hard, otherwise, Mom hits me. Got it! One way or another, someone's getting walloped.*

I follow my Mom downstairs to wait for the inevitable.

Fury

I'm ten years old and at the marl hole playing with my friends after school. Harry, a chestnut tatter's horse, is tethered to a stake with a long rope. My friends and I are pulling up juicy-looking weeds and grasses to feed him. "Here you are, Harry. Have some fresh greens," I say, stroking him on the neck.

Out of the corner of my eye I see Alan Rhodes and his posse approaching. They are all 18 to 21 years old. With their bushy sideburns and slicked-back hair, they look like a group of shabby Elvis impersonators. Alan walks up to me and glances at Harry. "He looks pretty friendly with you. You wanna have a go at riding him?"

"How am I gonna ride him? He doesn't have a saddle or reins."

"You don't need them if you hang onto his mane. It's what the Indians did," he says, nodding his head convincingly.

"How am I gonna get on him?" I ask, with visions of Little Joe Cartwright galloping through my mind.

"I'll help you up, and we'll just walk you 'round a little bit," he reassures me.

"Don't do it!" Smithy interjects, looking skeptically at the older boys. "How you gonna steer him?"

"It's okay," Alan insists. "You can have a go next. Like I said, I'll just lead him around." He lifts me onto the horse. "Now, hang onto his mane." He unties Harry's rope and leads us to an open area.

A rush of adrenaline and pride surges through me and I confidently grab a chunk of the horse's mane. I feel like Geronimo, sitting on the horse's bare back and feeling his weight shift beneath me when I'm startled by a loud smack behind me.

"Yahhh!!" Alan screams as he wallops Harry on the arse with a switch. Harry spooks and takes off galloping down the path toward Toll End Road. As he runs, he turns his head back toward me, whinnying and showing his teeth. It occurs to me that he might think I was the one who hit him.

I grab his mane with both hands and squeeze my legs around his sides, trying to hang on. "Whoa, Harry, whoa! It wasn't me!" Harry lowers his head and picks up speed. I'm sure he'll stop when he reaches the main road, but instead the cars screech to a halt as Harry barrels across the street toward the coal yard.

Pedestrians scatter, shouting obscenities at my recklessness. "You crazy bastard!" one man hollers, coming out of the pub. He tries to follow me but is quickly left in the dust.

Harry knows where he's going. He skirts the coal yard through the alleyway, nearly decapitating me with a tree branch. Then he hangs a sharp left toward the entrance to the power station and it takes me a few seconds to pull myself to the center of his back again. His metal horseshoes clatter loudly on the pavement, and the guard at the power station tries to get me to stop.

"Whoa! What the hell!" he shouts as the horse hangs a sharp right around him to head down the canal tow path.

Fisherman scatter and curse as we blaze past. I think about jumping off into the water in the hopes that Harry won't follow me. But Harry takes us over the canal bridge and slams my leg into the railing, trying to get me off. The next time he veers toward the railing, I lift my leg out of the way and lie almost flat across his back. Harry looks back at me, snorts, and tears off toward the coke banks. These are 30- to 40-foot-high piles of tennis-ball-sized pieces of coke, used to fuel the power generators.

I'm not sure what Harry has in mind, but I'm getting the impression that our friendship is over. He swings close along the coke bank, and I take my chance and dive off, intending to quickly climb up out of his reach. Instead I sink into the side of the bank.

Watching Harry gallop away, I feel a sense of relief. Then he turns around and heads back toward me at full speed. I roll over onto all fours and scramble madly upwards, but I'm just digging myself into the coke. I hear Harry's hooves getting closer. Dripping with sweat, my heart pounding, I realize the only way for me to climb the bank is to move extremely slowly. Repressing every natural instinct, I start to climb, carefully distributing my weight between my hands and feet. I hear Harry snorting, and expect to feel his hooves smash down on my back at any moment.

Harry's hooves crash into the coke right below my feet, and I slip down a few inches. I look over my shoulder and see his front legs have sunk deep into the bank. Baring his teeth, snorting, and huffing, he backs up and tries to slam me again. I continue my agonizingly slow ascent, moving away from the raging beast that used to be Harry, and I'm reminded of Bunjy.

After a few attempts to climb the bank, Harry backs away and begins pacing up and down, glaring at me. I realize I'm safe for the moment and I sit on the coke bank watching him. He wanders a few hundred feet away to munch on some grass and I start to inch my way down the bank. But the crunching of the coke beneath me alerts him and he runs straight at me. I do my slow-motion scramble back up the bank.

Two hours later, I'm still perched on the coke bank and Harry has wandered off again. I sneak down and dash toward the canal, ready to dive in if I have to. Thankfully, when I look over my shoulder, he's not there.

About a week later, Johnny, who looks a lot like me, runs into the kitchen crying and screaming and holding one side of his arse. He says that he was walking across the marl hole from school when Harry came charging toward him. Johnny dropped his books and ran, but Harry caught him at the edge of the tip, bit him on the arse, and flung him over the side.

Johnny pulls his trousers down revealing the biggest hicky I have ever seen, with a perfect set of horse teeth prints on his right arse cheek.

Bunjy is annoyed. "What did you do to Harry to get him after you like that?"

Scruffy

It's lunch time at Great Bridge School. Six girls are playing jump rope and one of them is Madelyn Pinkosky, my first crush. With her delicate features and silky, honey-blonde hair, she reminds me of Lady Penelope in one of my favorite TV shows, Thunderbirds. She smiles a lot and wears nice clothes. I can only wonder what her life is like.

I walk past the girls, catching a brief glimpse of Madelyn, who is jumping rope. I hear the girls singing, "Kiss the prince or Scruffy McCandless, the prince or Scruffy McCandless…" This goes on until Madelyn trips on "Scruffy McCandless."

"Madelyn, now you have to kiss Scruffy! And here he is!" they shout, pushing her toward me and laughing. Madelyn's sweet face goes bright red as she stands before me in my old, hand-me-down clothes and tattered shoes. "Go on Madelyn, give your man a hug!" her friend Linda urges.

"I'm sorry," Madelyn says quietly, looking me in the eyes, then shifting her gaze downward. I'm hoping she doesn't notice the holes in my shoes.

"I-I-It's okay. I'm sorry, too."

The moment is interrupted by a loud "Oy, Scruffy!" It's Alan Grubb, mocking my predicament. I'm grateful for the opportunity to belt someone. I run at him, and he takes off toward the water fountain where his mates hang out. Catching him by the shirt, I wallop him up the side of the head. Robert Perry, one of Alan's posse, grabs me by the hair and kicks me in the shin.

"Get him!" Alan shouts, and they all lunge for me. I push Alan into the gang of boys and throw a right hook onto Perry's chin. Perry hits the ground, the class bell rings, and we all race to the roll call assembly area.

The headmaster, Mr. Knock, is a short, balding, well-fed man with brown, horn-rimmed glasses. His shirt and tie always look like they're squeezing his neck. We call him Knocky.

"Robert Perry!" Knocky barks. There is no answer. "Perry! I know you were here for lunch. Speak up, boy!" Still no answer.

Knocky directs Mr. Beadle to walk his class line. Beadle shakes his head.

"Does anybody know where Perry is? Put your hand up if you do!" Knocky orders.

"Tony McCandless knocked him out, sir," Alan shouts from two lines over.

"What! Knocked him out?" Knocky's eyebrows rise over his glasses. "Where is he?"

"He's lying on the floor by the drinking fountain, sir."

Mr. Beadle grabs me by the scruff of my neck and drags me round the corner, followed by a procession of teachers and students. Sure enough, there is Perry, still lying on the ground, out cold. He's flat on his back with one knee bent, and he looks to be in a peaceful sleep.

A couple of teachers bring Perry around, sit him up, and give him some water. They escort him to the nurse, while Mr. Beadle leads me to Knocky's office.

"What did you hit him with?" Mr. Knock asks. He folds his hands on his desk and leans toward me.

"What do you think I hit him with? My fist," I say, showing him my knuckles.

"You're telling me you hit him with your fist? You didn't use a stick or a rock?"

"No, sir. Ask the other kids."

"I don't believe it." Knocky shakes his head. "Perry has a good-sized bruise on his chin. It's important you tell the truth; you're in a lot of trouble."

"I am telling the truth."

He glances over at Mr. Beadle, who shrugs his shoulders. Knocky glares at me from behind his desk. "Why did you leave him on the floor? Do you realize he could have died?"

"I had no idea he was out. I hit him just as the bell rang, and I ran to roll call with everybody else."

The headmaster walks us out of his office and sends Mr. Beadle back to his class. While I wait in the hall, Knocky checks on Perry in the nurse's office. "Luckily, Robert appears to be okay," he says. "But, you can't be running around bullying people and belting them like that. Now, come in my office." He gets his bamboo switch and grabs my wrist, then smacks the palm of each hand three times. I know from experience to keep my thumb out of the way, 'cause I don't need a bruised thumb on top of a stinging hand.

Knocky frowns. "Go back to your class now. I'll send for you later."

I step into the bathroom and run warm water over my stinging hands.

Later, Mr. Knock calls me into his office and hands me an envelope. "Be sure your parents get that. I want to see them here." He gives me a stern look.

Yeah, right, I think, stuffing the letter in my trouser pocket.

A few days later, I'm in class and my teacher, Mr. Plant, tells me to report to the headmaster's office.

"What for?"

"Never mind what for, just go. Leave your work on the desk."

Mr. Knock calls me into his office. When I enter, Robert Perry's parents are sitting, with their arms folded, on a couple of chairs placed across from three empty chairs. They look me up and down disapprovingly and then cast each other a knowing glance.

Robert's mother turns to me. "So you're Scruffy McCandless! You hooligan!" she rants. "What did you hit my Robert with?"

"Now, hold on a minute," Mr. Knock protests. "No name calling." He turns to me. "Where are your parents?"

"I don't know where they are," I reply. Then I realize I still have his letter in my trouser pocket.

I sit quietly as Robert's parents unload on me, but I don't understand what I've done wrong. Alan and his friends jumped me, and I smacked Perry fair and square.

I'm not sorry.

When I get home, I tell my mom what happened and hand her Knocky's note. She reads it and purses her lips. "You ay done nothin' wrong. Headmaster Knock shouldn't have caned you for standing up for yourself!"

The following day there is a commotion at school. Bunjy has ridden his bike over to "meet" with Headmaster Knock. After beating him around his office and leaving him unconscious, Bunjy places the crumpled note on his desk, and rides away before the cops arrive.

From then on, the teachers and staff at Great Bridge School no longer harass me. I guess this incident filled in the picture for them.

Time with Colin

Smithy's older brother Alfie is walking across the marl hole carrying their little brother, Colin, who is seven years old. Colin is out cold, his head and feet dangling over Alfie's arms. I ask Smithy what happened, and he tells me Colin fell down the tip and got knocked out.

As the weeks go by Colin gets sick and is diagnosed with cancer. The doctors think it was caused by the fall since Colin was perfectly fit before that.

I see Colin out front with his tricycle. His belly is swollen and he has trouble peddling. I push him around the paths and he giggles. "Be careful, Tony," Colin's mom reminds me. "He's been looking forward to this, but make sure he doesn't fall."

"Don't worry," I say. "Colin's a good driver." We toodle around until Colin gets tired and asks me to take him back into the house.

Over the weeks this gets to be a regular activity for us. Each time I see him, his face, arms, and legs are thinner.

Sometimes Colin asks me to set up his Johnny 7 machine gun, which he loves. I assemble it for him and he pulls the trigger, which launches grenades and fires caps. All the kids want one, but no one can afford it. When we get the gun out, the kids gather around. Colin enjoys the attention and lets them all have a try.

Because they're terraced houses, there is only a single wall between Colin's bedroom and mine. Most nights I listen to him crying and moaning in pain. His belly is growing bigger by the day and he is getting weaker. The doctors say there is no cure. I wish there was something someone could do.

Private Property

Smithy and I are collecting parts to build a go-kart. We find an old pram at the marl hole and scavenge the axles and wheels. All we need now is a good plank to sit on.

My uncle Andy, who is married to my mom's younger sister Floss takes us over to the building site on the west side of the marl hole where three 12-story public housing buildings are under construction. He works as a scaffolder there. Andy is wiry with a medium build. He has an open face with large eyes and long, brown hair. He seems happy and smiles a lot.

Andy introduces me to the carpenter foreman and I ask him if he has an old plank we could have. He shows me a pile of scrap wood and says we can have anything we want off that pile, but not to touch the stacked wood. Unfortunately, in the scrap pile there is nothing long enough for our go-kart, but I do get some free firewood.

It's Saturday morning and I'm waiting for Smithy to come over so we can check the scrap woodpile for a decent plank. He's late, so I decide to knock on his door. As I open the gate, I hear Colin howling with pain. I figure Smithy is trying to console him and decide to go to the woodpile on my own.

There is a hole in the chain-link fence and I slip through and head to the woodpile. No one seems to be working today and the site is eerily quiet. I sort through the wood and spot a damaged scaffold plank. *Perfect!* I can cut off the broken end and it will still be long enough.

"Hey, what are you doing?" a uniformed security guard with a big German Shepard looms over me. He is medium height, podgy, and pasty faced. Long, black, greasy hair sticks out from under his American-cop-style hat. He looks like an overstuffed sausage roll in his tan uniform.

"I-I-I'm sorting myself a plank out. T-T-Tom the carpenter foreman said I could have anything off this pile."

His eyes narrow and he takes a step toward me. "I don't believe that for one minute. You're stealing wood. How old are you?"

"T-T-Ten."

The dog is tugging at his leash. "Sit, Spitz!" The dog sits next to the guard's leg. "Don't be running off, 'cause I'll have to set him on you and you won't outrun him." He smirks.

"I've done n-n-nothing wrong. I'm just g-g-getting some scrap wood," I insist, stepping away from the pile.

"You'll have to come with me to the office and I'll take some notes. Follow me." He leads me into a partially constructed building and up a key-access freight elevator to the top. I look over the edge and see the ground a hundred feet below.

"You know, if you were up here and Spitz was chasing you, you could fall off of this building and there'd be nothing I could do about it." He eyes me like a cat watching a caged bird.

"That's okay. I don't come up here," I say, trying to keep my distance and looking for an escape route.

He steps toward me with the dog. "Let's get over to the office and I'll take down your name and address." We go back down to a trailer near Spring Street. He puts the dog in the trailer and closes the door. "Come on," he says, pointing to another door, "we're going in here."

"No, we're not!" I seize my opportunity and dash out onto the road toward home. I spot my mother coming across the marl hole with groceries.

"What's the hurry?" she says, "Here, give me a hand with these bags."

I explain what happened and what the guard said. Mom listens, pursing her lips. "Did he lay his hands on you?"

"No. I ran away when he tried to get me into his office." We take the groceries into the house.

"Come and show me where this office is at." She is getting her wild-eyed look. We walk to the building site and see the guard approaching with his dog.

"Hey, missus, you can't be over here. This is private property."

My mom marches right up to him and punches him in the face, knocking his fancy hat off. "You sick bastard!" she shouts, peppering him with blows. He lets go of Spitz, who whines and scampers out of the way.

"What are you doing scaring a ten-year old boy like that?" she yells. "I'll get the real cops on you, you weird bastard! What are you, some kind of molester?"

"Just trying to do my job, missus," he whimpers, backing away.

Mom stomps on his hat and grinds a muddy heel into it. "You keep away from the kids!" Then she grabs me by the arm and walks us right back through the site and toward home. I'm bursting with pride.

"Don't be coming over here on the weekends," she warns. "If you need wood, come in the week when there's people around."

"Okay, Mom. Thanks for sorting him out. He wasn't so tough after all! And how about his guard dog, more like the cowardly lion!" I chuckle, grateful that it was someone else who got the walloping today.

Bag of Marbles

I'm playing marbles with Smithy on the side of my house and I'm losing. He has to go in for tea and says he'll be back shortly. "I'll give you a chance to win these back after my sandwich." He smiles.

A while later Smithy comes out. He has tears in his eyes. "What's a matter?" I ask. "You're winning."

He hands me his bag of marbles. "Here, have 'em. I don't want 'em." He leans on the wall, hanging his head. Tears are running down his cheeks.

"What's wrong?"

"I think Colin just died. Alfie's running over to the phone box to call the ambulance. But it's no use. I think he's gone."

I'm breathless and unable to speak. I put my arm around him and feel him sobbing.

Alfie comes back from the phone box, grabs Smithy by the hand, and takes him inside. I sit alone against the wall, staring at Smithy's bag of marbles. I think about the last time I pushed Colin on his tricycle, the last time I saw him alive. It feels strange to think I'm living in a world where a kid like Colin could suffer like that. How can there be a God? And if there is, why doesn't he care about what's going on at the marl hole?

Nine Lives

I've had my cat, Jimmy, a few years now. A neighbor gave him to me as a kitten, and I've been paying for his food with money I earn doing odd jobs. He's a tabby tom with bright green eyes. Mom puts up with him because he earns his keep catching rats and mice, which are in no short supply from the marl hole.

I'm in the front room and hear my mother yelling at the top of the stairs. Bunjy is not home, so I look to see what's going on. Mom glares down at me. "Your damn cat is up here again!" she explodes. "I told you to keep him down there, away from the baby!"

She has my cat, Jimmy, by the scruff of his neck and is opening the window at the top of the stairs. "I'll teach him!" she hisses.

"No! Don't!" I shout, rushing toward her as she hurls him out the window. I envision him impaled on the pointed metal fence that separates our house from the marl hole, and I burst out the front door, but am relieved to see Jimmy scampering across the marl hole. He doesn't appear to be hurt; he must have landed on his feet. I run after him, calling him, but he doesn't come back.

I run back in the house and upstairs to my mom. "Why'd you do that? You could have killed him!"

"Good! The next time I catch him up here, I won't be so nice!" Mom snarls, slamming the window shut.

It's evening and I'm looking for Jimmy. I find him at the marl hole. "Here, Jimmy. Come here, boy." I pick him up, check him over, and carry him back to the house to feed him. I put him down outside the kitchen step and go inside to get his can of food when he shoots right back through the fence to his new home, the marl hole.

Although he continues to let me feed and pet him over the months, he never again sets foot in our house.

Fan Tails and Tumblers

Mr. Yates, the neighbor at the bottom of our garden, keeps pigeons in a huge, raised pen. He flies them twice a day and they shit all over our slate roofs. He is a grumpy, old bastard who wears a waistcoat over a shirt with the sleeves rolled up to his elbows. Sometimes I see him at the pigeon pen. From the back, his thinning wreath of grey hair frames the speckled, uneven crown of his head.

I'm always looking for ways to earn a few shillings, and I think I could manage cleaning his pens. "What kind of pigeons are those?" I ask.

"What do you care? You could never afford them or a pen like this," he scoffs, tossing a handful of seed with his stubby, nicotine-stained fingers. I persist and eventually he tells me he's got some Fan Tails, and Tumblers, which he breeds and sells. His favorite is a light grey Fan Tail he's named Gorgeous George. He has black bands across his back and a shimmery green head. Mr. Yates has had Gorgeous George for a while and he has sold many of his offspring.

It's been a few days since my conversation with Mr. Yates and I'm looking for my cat, Jimmy. He sometimes disappears for a while, but he always comes back and visits me. I'm feeding my remaining chickens when I notice Jimmy halfway through the paling fence at the top of our garden. He is perfectly still with his green eyes open, and as I walk up to him I wonder why he is not meowing his usual greeting.

When I touch him, he's as stiff as a board. I look over the fence and see four more cats lying dead in the grass and under the pigeon pen. I realize the old bastard must have poisoned them.

I'm pulling Jimmy out of the fence when Mr. Yates comes around the pigeon pen. "W-W-What did you do? D-D-Did you poison my cat?"

"Poison? I don't use poison. What do you mean?" he smirks. "What's all these dead cats doing here? Good. Bastard cats are always worrying my pigeons."

I feel a blackness come over me and I'm overwhelmed by the urge to jump the fence and bash his head in. I watch him saunter back into his pigeon pen. Holding poor Jimmy, stiff and silent in my hands, I hear him talking to his cooing pigeons. At that moment, I imagine his pigeon pen blazing and all his prized birds going up in smoke.

I carry Jimmy into the house and find Mom in the kitchen. "Jimmy's dead." I say, holding him up.

"How'd that happen?"

"I think Mr. Yates poisoned 'im."

"Well, how do you know *he* poisoned him?" she asks, looking up from cutting carrots.

"There's four of Annie's cats lying dead in his yard, too. He's killed 'em all."

"Well, what do you expect me to do?" she says without emotion. "Wait till Bunjy gets home and we'll tell him about it." *Yeah, right.* I grab the shovel from the coal place and walk out to the marl hole to bury Jimmy.

Phillip cackles when he sees my cat. "You could use him as a tennis racquet!" The other kids laugh at Jimmy's stiff body, still in a walking position. I tell them where to go, and then find a grassy spot where I hope the dogs will not dig him up, and I lay Jimmy to rest.

I pop home, grab our paraffin can, and walk across the marl hole to the hardware store. "You want more paraffin already?" Mr. Collins asks.

"Yes." I hand him the can.

"Gallon?"

"Yes."

"It's gonna be a cold night," he says as he pours the paraffin.

"Not at my house."

It's just gone dark and I'm sitting in Mr. Yates's garden, under his pigeon pen. I have crumpled the pages of some Express and Star newspapers and have matches and paraffin. I imagine myself standing in our yard, watching the blaze, and seeing Mr. Yates madly rushing around trying to save his precious pigeons. I know this will be a big blaze, but I reckon it is far enough away from the brick houses and slate roofs to be safe.

I picture the crowds of neighbors, the blaring fire engines, and the look of shock on Mr. Yates's face. I want to be close enough to hear him say, "What happened? Who did this to my pigeons?" I'm sure the pen will be burnt to the ground before the fire engines even get close. If I'm questioned by the police, I'll say, "Maybe it was the same person who poisoned the cats."

I've been sitting under the pigeon pen now for over an hour thinking of all the possible scenarios and letting the rush of satisfaction I will feel give me momentary relief from my rage. It's dark and all I can hear is the soft cooing of the pigeons above me as they settle in for the night. I see kitchen lights going out as people move to their front rooms and settle by the fire. I'm shivering and don't know if it's from the cold or adrenaline. I probably should be worried about getting caught, but the satisfaction will be worth it, consequences be damned! Mr. Yates may never know who, but he will know why.

With my back to Mr. Yates's house, I open the box of Swan Vesta wooden matches, pull one out, and strike it on the side of the box. The red match tip hisses to life and momentarily illuminates me and my incriminating paraphernalia. Then the bright orange flame makes everything around it look blacker.

It occurs to me that the blaze will get going more quickly if I stuff the newspapers into the wooden crates next to me and pour paraffin on them. I blow out the match and get everything set. I calculate my escape route with the fuel can and pull out another match.

I can't help thinking of the pigeons. They've done nothing. I imagine the mothers flapping around in the flames trying to protect their squabs and nests. Then I think about poor Jimmy in his last moments, trying to squeeze through the fence and come home, and that bastard Mr. Yates getting what he deserves.

I light the match and stare into the flame, watching it flicker and sway down the match stick. For a moment, I feel quiet inside. The heat of the flame reaches my fingers and I blow out the match. I sit in the cold darkness for a few minutes, and then I have a better idea. I grab the fuel can and the matches and jump back over the fence.

The next morning I get up early and make sure I'm feeding my chickens at the bottom of the garden when Mr. Yates comes to let out his pigeons. Right away he notices the stacked wooden crates, stuffed with crumpled, paraffin-soaked paper, and figures out that someone has set up to burn down his pigeon pen.

"What the hell! Who's been under here!" he shouts, picking up a half-burnt match. He rushes back to his kitchen and brings his wife out. "Look! Look! Someone's tried to set a fire. Someone's trying to burn my pen down!" Mrs. Yates covers her mouth and shrieks.

I throw more corn to my chickens and quietly watch the spectacle.

"What do you know about this?" Mr. Yates barks at me across the fence. "Have you been over here setting fires?"

"No, not me. I'm just feeding my chickens." I smile. "Somebody around here really doesn't like animals."

For many months after that, Mr. Yates and his wife would come out during the night with flashlights, checking for whoever it was to come back and finish the job. That was revenge enough for me.

Another Hole

I'm in the back yard throwing bread crumbs to my chickens and I see our neighbor Mr. Mole digging in his garden. His lot backs up to the marl hole at the top of ours. "Those chickens are looking plump," he teases, leaning his stocky frame on his garden fork. He has a broad, Irish face with a mop of wooly, auburn curls.

"Don't you start. These are my last two."

"What happened to the others?"

"My dad ate 'em."

Mr. Mole's thoughtful, green eyes gaze quietly at me for a moment. "Well, what did you expect?"

"I know, but I'm done after these."

"Why don't you plant some vegetables in that patch of dirt you've got there? Maybe he'll leave your chickens alone for a while. You've got chicken manure."

"What kind of vegetables?"

"Well, you can plant anything this time of year. That's what I'm doing. Here, I've got some seeded spuds. I'll give you some." He walks over to his shed to get them, and I run into the coal place and grab the shovel.

When I return, he looks at me and smiles. "What are you hoping to do with that?"

"Dig the garden."

He laughs. "That's a coal shovel, not a spade. You'll just bounce off that clay soil. Here, use this." He hands me a garden fork over the fence. "You can keep that. I've got a new one."

"Really?"

"But I want to see that garden dug. You'll need to dig it all over, then turn it back, and make your furrows. You plant your spuds twelve inches apart in the high soil, so they'll drain. Spuds don't like to have wet feet." He hands me the tray of seeded spuds.

"Thank you, Mr. Mole," I say, excited about my new venture into vegetable farming.

"You've got some work to do. I'm going in for a cuppa. I'll come out later to see how you're doing." Mr. Mole disappears into his house and I start digging.

I've been toiling for a while now and have turned the soil over. It's getting late, and I want to get the spuds planted. My arms are feeling heavy and I'm tired. I glance over to see if Mr. Mole is back in his yard as I thrust the fork into the ground and feel it hit something hard. I look down and see my left shoe wedged between the first and third fork prongs, with the second prong embedded in my foot. I glance toward the house to see if Bunjy is watching. Relieved that he is not, I try to pull the fork out, but my shoe is jammed between the prongs and I nearly pull myself over.

I'm yanking frantically and hopping around like a deranged Morris dancer. In my mind, I hear Bunjy shouting, "Idjit!" To an onlooker, it might appear that he is right.

Exhausted, I decide to try a new tack. Leaning on the pitch fork still in my foot to keep my balance, I step on the toes of the skewered foot with my free foot to hold it down. I'm really hoping Mr. Mole doesn't come out right now. With one slow, strong pull, I manage to free the fork.

I sit down and remove my shoe, wondering how I'm going to explain this to Bunjy. There is a hole in my foot that, to my surprise, is not bleeding much. Luckily the prong pierced between the bones. I put my shoe back on, slip into the house, and call my mom over.

"Mom, I need a bandaid for my foot."

"Now what you done?" She looks at the hole in my foot, puzzled. "How'd you do that?"

"I stuck my garden fork into it."

"What garden fork?"

"The one Mr. Mole gave me. I've dug the back garden over for spuds."

My mom takes a closer look at the wound. "Your toes seem okay, but you may need a tetanus shot. Your dad's going to have to take you up to the hospital."

"Tetanus shot?" Bunjy interrupts. "Who needs a tetanus shot?" Mom explains what happened.

"Idjit! You're supposed to dig the ground, not your foot! Where'd you get the fork? Did you pinch it?" he growls, reaching for my shoe to inspect it.

"Mr. Mole gave it to me. "

"He did, did he. Look, now you've got another hole in your shoe!" He smacks me on the head with my dirty shoe.

On the way to the hospital Bunjy sits silently next to me on the bus. For a moment I picture him saying, "Never mind, son, good effort, accidents happen." He turns around, sees me looking up at him, and barks, "What?"

"Nothing." The bus rolls on.

Joyful Children

My friend Smithy and I are out playing on the marl hole having a marl clay war. We're making a pile of egg-sized balls of clay. We have discovered that we can accurately throw the clay twice as far using a 3-foot switch as we can with our hands.

"Get ready!" I pop my head up and shout to our opponents, Phillip and Keith, who are hunkered down behind a mound of dirt and rubbish. They respond with a barrage of mustard-yellow missiles.

A sticky wad slaps the side of my head. "You bastards! We're not ready yet." I duck for cover and load up my stick.

"Hey!" Smithy shouts underneath a hailstorm of clay. "They've got two more kids with them. We're outnumbered!" We return fire and manage to score a couple of hits. We're almost out of ammo when my brothers Johnny and Dave see our predicament and join the cause.

"Johnny, grab a switch!" I shout. "Dave, make some ammo!" Smithy beans one of Phillip's team in the face, and the boy scampers off bleating.

I peek over the mound and see Bunjy in our back garden, looking our way. "Hold fire, Bunjy's spotted us." His loud whistle pierces the air, calling us home, and the last kid back is guaranteed a thick lug. Johnny and Dave are already racing toward the house, so I take my time, feeling like some sort of masochistic Pavlov's dog.

"Why didn't you run?" Bunjy prods. "You know the last one back gets a thick lug."

"What's the point? They're faster than I am." I admit. "I'm gonna get a thick lug anyway."

"Go get me some Senior Service cigarettes from Willis."

I deliver the cigarettes to my dad and walk back outside when I feel something whiz past my head and splat on the wall behind me. A baby-poop-yellow blob of clay about the size of a fried egg is stuck to the side of our house. I try to scrape it off with my fingernails, but it's embedded in the stucco and gravel finish.

"Hey, quit that!" I scold "This stuff doesn't come off!" I immediately regret having said this.

"Oh, that's too bad," Phillip mocks. Within seconds, a hailstorm of clay is splattering on the side of our house. I race over to Phillip and yank his switch out of his hand just as Bunjy saunters out, smoking a cigarette. He looks up at the wall and stops mid-drag, then turns and sees me with a switch in my hand. Phillip and his gang take off.

"Get over here! Look at the mess you've made," Bunjy barks. He snatches my switch and tries to get the clay off the side of the house. "This ain't coming off!" he mumbles through clenched teeth. "What were you thinking, you idjit?" He wallops me, grabs me by the collar, and drags me into the house.

Mom jumps in. "What's going on now? Leave him alone!"

"You get to your bed and stay there," he orders, shoving me toward the stairs. "Joyce, have a look at the side of the house." Mom steps outside, followed by Bunjy. "Look at this mess," he grumbles.

"Oh, dear. Did he do all that?" I overhear through the upstairs window.

"I saw him with a switch in his hand."

"What was he thinking?"

"As usual, he wasn't. Little retard," Bunjy snaps.

It's been an hour since my dad sent me to my room. I'm staring at the cracked ceiling, listening to the kids playing outside in the warm afternoon sun. Knowing I'm here for the night, I roll over and try to get to sleep. The grueling boredom is interrupted by a pinging sound on my window. I sit up and hear it again. "Tone! Tone!" Smithy is calling. I decide to ignore it, hoping he will stop before he draws Bunjy's attention.

Unfortunately, he persists. I listen carefully to make sure Bunjy's not already coming up the stairs, then I tiptoe to the window, trying to avoid the creaky floor boards. I spot Smithy gathering another handful of gravel. Waving my arms, I mouth, "Stop it! Stop it!"

As he gets ready to throw another handful, he sees me in the window and freezes, wide-eyed, which I take as a bad sign. Smithy drops the gravel and runs. I turn to see Bunjy has materialized behind me.

"When I tell you to stay in bed, you stay in bed!" Bunjy slaps me around the bedroom and I get well acquainted with the floorboards and walls. I'm relieved when he finally throws me on my bed and goes downstairs. I lie there quietly. The ringing in my ears helps drown out the sound of the joyful children playing outside.

Wooden Stake

It's been a few days since Smithy threw pebbles at my window, and I can't help but wonder how Bunjy can sneak up the creaky, bare wooden stairs without making a sound. I'm on the stairs in my socks trying to figure it out. I try all fours, tiptoes, skipping steps, and walking on the side rails, with no success.

I decide to focus my efforts on ways to get down the stairs quietly. The last two steps are especially noisy, so I jump off the third one and land softly at the bottom. *That works. I'm on to something!* I move up and jump off the sixth step without too much noise. Step number eight works well, so I think, *Damn it, I'll go for it!*

Feeling pumped, I take a flying leap off the top step in a daredevil attempt to clear all thirteen steps. My flight path is interrupted by the ground floor ceiling, where it opens up for the stairs. My forehead slams into the wall and my feet swing up until my body is parallel with the staircase. After a Wile E. Coyote moment, I drop onto the back of my head and shoulders and thump my way down the last five steps. Lying in a heap at the bottom, I decide to scratch this off my list of stealthy ways to get down the stairs.

The door from the living room bursts open and Bunjy's there with my mom looking over his shoulder, wide-eyed. "What the bloody hell was all that noise? You scared your mother half to death!" He looks down at me. "What did you do?"

Since I can't disclose the true nature of my activities, I tell him I fell down the stairs. Bunjy looks at me puzzled. "What was that bang, then? We heard a loud bang before you hit the stairs. Where'd you slip from?"

"The top step," I say.

Bunjy is not convinced. "He's been being a bloody idjit again! God knows what he was up to." Bunjy stares intently at me. "He probably tried to jump down the stairs and bumped his head on the ceiling."

I look at him surprised.

"He could have broke his neck!" He drags me up by my shirt and wallops me on the back of my head, apparently already having forgotten about the possibility of the broken neck. "Get to bed, idjit!" he growls, shoving me up the stairs.

Lying in bed with a stiff neck, I can't help but feel uneasy that not only can Bunjy hypnotize chickens and materialize from nowhere, but he also appears to be able to read minds and fly up the stairs. I wonder if I will need a wooden stake to resolve this situation.

Some Bonce!

It's dark and I'm outside looking for Smithy. I feel a smack on the back of my head and see Johnny and David race past. "Hey, slowpoke!"

I chase after them and as usual they tease me by letting me almost catch them, then sprinting away effortlessly. I'm not as fast as they are but I can run long distances, and I chase them in the hope that they will eventually tire.

After a few minutes, I follow Johnny around a large, parked lorry, hear a loud bong, and the lights go out. Johnny looks over his shoulder just in time to see my feet flying toward him.

I awake with a start. "What the hell!" I'm lying on my back with my arse in the curb and my feet on the sidewalk, looking up at a blurry streetlight. Five pairs of legs surround me. Thinking someone must have hit me with a rounders bat, I let out a barrage of expletives and try to get up and fight back.

"Tsk! Tsk! Listen to his language!" Old Lady Ferris scoffs, tightening her woolen shawl around her shoulders. "It's disgraceful! He's swearing like a sailor." She turns to her daughter, Anne. "Leave him lie there and come back in the house."

I hear her voice above me. "Tony, it's me Anne Ferris, you need to lie still!"

"Who the hell hit me?" I sputter.

Johnny kneels beside me and grabs my arms. "Tony, lie still. Nobody hit you. You ran into a steel H-beam sticking off

97

the back of the lorry. I felt it touch my hair as I went under it. We knocked on Anne's door when we saw you weren't moving."

"Mom, he's been out for a while; we need to help him," Anne insists. "Go get a damp towel from the house."

Mrs. Ferris returns, sour-faced, with the towel. "Isn't that one of that drunken Irishman's kids from the marl hole? Go fetch him. He can deal with it."

"Not now, Mom. I think Tony has a concussion." Anne folds the damp towel and places it on my forehead. It feels good. "He should probably go to the hospital."

"Let me get up." I clamber onto my knees and Smithy reaches me his hand.

"I heard somebody tried to bend a steel beam with his head," he says, smiling. "I guessed it was you!"

"Bollocks, Smithy!" I pull myself to my feet. The towel falls to the ground, revealing a purple stripe just below the hair line on my badly swollen forehead.

"Wow!" Smithy gasps. "That's some bonce! You could be on Star Trek!"

The Ferrises go indoors, and the relentless ribbing about my expanding dome continues on the walk home.

"What's a concussion?" David asks.

"It means a giant, oversized head," Smithy chortles as he leaves us at our back door.

We walk in the kitchen. "Mom, Tony knocked himself out," Johnny announces. Luckily, Bunjy is not home.

"What? Not again! Let me see." She inhales sharply. "Oh dear! That's swollen. Does it hurt?"

"Only when you press it like that."

"Sorry. I'll run a towel under the cold tap." She hands me the towel. "Hold that on your head and we'll see how it is in the morning." Mom sends me to bed.

The next day my parents are too busy to take me to the hospital.

The Man in a Dress

It's Saturday morning and our bellies are full of tea and crusty loaf toast slathered with salty butter. I'm looking out the front window, waiting for Smithy to come over, when I spot a hefty, grey-haired stranger approaching our house. Bunjy is sitting at the table sipping a mug of tea and reading the newspaper.

"Dad, there's a man outside in a long, black dress!"

Bunjy looks at me, puzzled, and gets up just as there is a loud rap at the door. He marches over and flings it open. My dad and the stranger size each other up.

"Good morning, Mr. McCandless," the ruddy-faced man says in his Irish brogue.

"Don't be coming here knocking my door like the bloody coppers!" Bunjy snarls. "Who do you think you are?" I move behind my dad to size up the man in the dress; he is easily as tall as Bunjy and has him by 30 pounds.

"I'm Father O'Reilly from St. Marks and I was hoping to see you in church tomorrow."

"Oh, that's what you're here for? The collection plate," Bunjy sneers. "Well, just because I have an Irish name and a bunch of kids doesn't make me a bloody Catholic! Where'd you get my name?" He steps toward the priest, and I'm thinking that the dress is not going to save the stranger, because I know Bunjy hits people in dresses.

"Oh, come now, Mr. McCandless, calm down. I'm just doing the Lord's work." The priest laces his fingers together in front of his chest. "What part of the old country are you from then?"

"Never mind where I'm from," Bunjy growls. "I've told you, I'm no Catholic and we'll have no popery here. Be on your way while you're safe!"

Bunjy steps back inside and slams the door behind him, shaking his head and gnashing his teeth. I look out the window and watch the priest leave, his long dress fluttering in the breeze. "What's a Catholic, Dad? And why is he wearing a dress?"

"It's nothing you need to worry about," Bunjy grunts, sitting back down to his newspaper and tea.

Calling in the Flocks

It's nine o'clock on Sunday morning. Mom is in the kitchen making breakfast for six of us kids who are already downstairs. Last night was a typical Saturday night in the McCandless household, and the old man is upstairs sleeping it off. The church bells are ringing as I sit down to a steaming cup of tea. I grab a slice of toast and dip it in my fried egg.

Suddenly Bunjy comes rushing down the stairs and bursts into the kitchen in his underpants. "For Christ's sake, Les, put yer trousers on!" Mom scolds.

"Where's me shirt?" he shouts from the toilet over his morning piss. This is followed by a loud, growling fart. The bathroom is practically in the kitchen, and most of the time he doesn't shut the door.

"It's drying on the bow, and do you have to be so noisy in there?" she snaps. I watch him march to the fireplace, pushing the younger kids out of the way. He pulls on his shirt and trousers. "Get me bike out of the coal place," he demands. "And where's me shoes?" I grab the bike and put it outside the kitchen door.

"They're in the bogey hole under the stairs," Mom says. Bunjy puts on his shoes, grabs a coat, and rushes out the door without another word.

"Is he going to work?" I ask Mom.

"No, it's Sunday. Never mind, we'll have breakfast in peace." She clears my plate from the table. "Give David your seat and go chop some wood for our Sunday fire."

An hour later, I'm still in the back yard cutting wood. Dad comes home and leans his bike against the wall outside. "Put this back in the coal hole," he orders.

"Do you want some tea and toast?" Mom asks.

"No, I'm going back to bed." He slips up the stairs and I wangle my way through the tangle of kids in the kitchen and put the bike away.

"Where's he been?" I ask.

"I don't know," Mom sighs. "Let him be."

I go back to cutting wood. A short time later, a police car pulls up in front of our house and two heavy-set uniformed cops get out. I poke my head in the kitchen.

"Mom, there's two coppers here!"

"Now, what!" she moans. I follow her to the front door.

"Morning, Missus. Does Les McCandless live here?" the older cop says.

"You know he does." She puts her hands on her hips. "What do you want?"

"Is he in?"

"He's upstairs in bed. Do you want me to get him up?"

"Yes, we need to talk to him." They stand ready, rocking on their heels.

"Les, a couple of coppers here for you!" Mom shouts up the stairs. She leaves the front door open and goes back to her housework. The old man comes down in his underwear, carrying his trousers.

"What do you want, waking me up on a Sunday morning?"

"Have you been up to St. Mark's Church this morning?"

"What? You can see you just got me up."

"It was reported that you rode up to church on a blue racer bike and attacked the bell ringer for 'making all that bloody noise on a Sunday morning when a man is trying to sleep.'"

"I don't know what you're talking about," Bunjy says with his best poker face.

The cops look at each other. "Get dressed! You need to come with us."

The neighbors peek out their windows as Bunjy is driven away in the back of the cop car.

I sit down next to my mother. "It sounds like he's been up and belted the bell ringer. You know, I can't hear any bells." I snicker.

"Oh, shut up," Mom scolds. "It ain't funny! We don't need any more trouble."

An hour later the cops bring Bunjy home.

He walks in the back door and Mom pounces. "What have you done now, you hungover Irish fool!"

"Och, shut up!" he bellows.

"Did you really wallop the bellringer? The News of the World will love this," she laments, referring to a gossipy neighbor two doors down. "Did they charge you with anything?"

"Och, never mind." He grabs his coat and leaves for the pub.

The house is quiet now, and I settle into the front room to draw a picture. As I sketch, I think about the bell ringer and wonder where his God was while Bunjy was thumping him for calling in the flocks.

Mongolian Idiots

It's been about three weeks since I bonged my head on the steel beam while chasing Johnny around a lorry in the dark. My forehead is still swollen and sore to the touch where the beam hit it.

Smithy and I are walking home past the Tipton cemetery. A light breeze pesters the leaves on the grass, which looks emerald green in the afternoon sun. Both of the big Victorian wrought iron cemetery gates are open. I run and jump on one and it swings a full 180 degrees to the stop on the other side. "Hey, this gate goes all the way 'round. We can have a ride!"

"Let me have a go!" Smithy yells. I hop off and let him jump on. Not wanting to miss out, I check out the other gate.

"Oh good, this one opens, too!" I pull out the ground pin and find to my delight that it swings more easily than the other gate.

"Okay, let's have a race!" I challenge. We pull our gates fully open, run, and jump on. "Come on, Smithy!" I shout with the wind in my hair.

At the closed position, my gate slams into the center stop, leaving only my head to continue the momentum. My forehead strikes the half-inch horizontal top rail of the gate—not above, not below, but in exactly the same place as the last collision. Seeing stars, I drop backwards onto the gravel drive.

Smithy sails past me. When he hears the crash, he jumps off and rushes over. Dazed, I first see his feet and legs, then take in his stupid grin. "Bloody hell, Tone, are you ok?" He bends down for a closer look. "Wow! You banged your head again! Let me help you up. You look like a dying fly with your legs in the air like that." Laughing nervously, he pulls me onto my feet.

"Jesus, Tone, you look like Herman Munster. All you need is a bolt in your neck!" He tilts his head, still studying me. "It looks a lot worse than the first time you did it."

I hang onto the gate with one hand and reach up with the other to feel my swollen, throbbing forehead. Smithy is laughing hysterically now. "You know it could have been worse."

"How?" I ask, gingerly touching my rapidly expanding forehead.

"It could have been me!" he chortles, moving out of striking range.

Smithy and I stiffen as the groundskeeper approaches on his bicycle. He is an elderly man who has chased us out of the cemetery many times before. I'm too dazed to make a run for it.

"I saw what happened, son. Are you ok?" He climbs off his bike and leans it against the gate. "You know you shouldn't be playing on these gates. Let me take a look at your head." He puts one hand on my shoulder and pushes my hair back with the other. His eyes grow wide behind his round metal-rimmed glasses.

"Dear me, kid, that's quite a bump. I'd say you've got a five-head now, not a forehead." He grins. Smithy bursts into nervous laughter, hopping around and shouting "Tony Five-head, Tony Five-head!" I watch him as the lump on my forehead begins to enter my line of vision.

"Now, now, don't tease him," the groundskeeper says. "I was just joking to try to make him feel better. Come with me and we'll get some cold water."

We walk across the path to a spigot next to a line of trash cans filled with dead flowers. The old man reaches into his coat, pulls out a handkerchief, and soaks it in cold water. I look at the handkerchief and wonder if it will stick to my forehead. "Never mind, it's clean," he says. "Now hold that on your head and wait here while I go get my works van. I'll take you over to the clinic and get that looked at."

He jumps on his bike and rides toward the parking lot.

"Smithy, I can't have him taking me home to Bunjy. He's told me not to play around the cemetery. I'll get a thick ear to match my swollen head." I hang the wet hanky on the spigot and we take off running through the graveyard in the opposite direction from the parking lot.

"That there is my granddad's grave," Smithy pants, " and that one—"

"Never mind the guided tour, Smithy. He could catch us on his bike if he sees us."

We dash out onto the canal bank and through the tar fields to Powis Avenue and home. I can hear Bunjy as we walk around to the back yard. "Hey, Smithy, do any of your brothers have a hat I could borrow?" My plan is to sneak in and go to bed and let my head get back to normal size before Bunjy sees it.

"They do," he says, grinning. "But even big Alfie's hat wouldn't fit that Frankenstein bonce!"

Johnny and David come flying out the back door. I grab Johnny by the arm. "Hey, Johnny, go and get my balaclava and bring it out here."

Johnny looks me in the face, puzzled. "What's wrong with your head?" He squints his eyes and tilts his head to one side. "You look weird."

"Never mind that, just go get me bloody hat!"

Johnny brings me the hat and has another look at my head. "Is your head broke? Is it gonna stay like that?" I put the hat on and roll the face of the balaclava up into a beany style, then pull it down to my eyebrows.

"How's that look, Smithy?" I ask hopefully.

"Whoa! Now you look even weirder. Your eyes are starting to swell shut. I'm going home before Bunjy gets started." He dives through the connecting yard gate and disappears into his kitchen.

I take a deep breath and push open the kitchen door. My mom is at the table with her back to me, and I see Bunjy sitting in the front room having a cup of tea. "Hey, Mom," I say, gliding past her and heading for the stairs.

"I've told you not to wear hats in the house. It's bad luck!" she snaps, yanking the balaclava off my head. "Sit down. I'll get you some tea."

Bunjy looks up at me. "What's wrong with your bloody face?" he shouts. He jumps up and grabs for me as I try to slip past him. "You been fighting again?" I tilt my throbbing head away from him. "Look at me when I'm talking to you!" He slaps me hard on my left ear, giving my sore brain another good rattle.

"Now what?" Mom shouts. "The kid just walked in and already you're slapping him around, you slap-happy bastard! Let him go! Leave him alone!"

"Look at his bloody head—and his eyes! Och, now he looks like a bloody Mongolian idjit!" He shakes his head. I squint up at him through my swollen eyes. My head is pounding in sync with the ringing in my ears, and I'm wondering how I will face the world looking like a Mongolian idiot.

Mom shoves Bunjy out of the way, turns me toward her, and shrieks, which I take as a bad sign. "Bloody hell, what happened?" she gasps. She leads me into the kitchen, gets a towel under the cold tap, and sits me down. "Here, hold that on your head."

I'm trying to come up with a story that doesn't involve the cemetery as Bunjy glares at me over Mom's shoulder. "Did somebody hit you with something? Who did it?" Mom asks. "The bastard!"

107

"No, no. I was chasing Smithy over the marl hole and I fell and bumped my head on a flat rock."

"Only that idiot could bump his head twice in the same place!" Bunjy shakes his head and goes back to his cup of tea.

"Oh, shut up! He's probably got a concussion. Look at him." Mom insists. "We're going to have to take him to the hospital."

"No!" Bunjy yells. "Leave him. He'll be okay. Put him to bed and we'll see how he is in the morning."

"It's all right Mom. I'll just go to bed. That cold towel feels good. I'm okay," I say, hoping to diffuse the tension and get away from Bunjy.

Mom follows me upstairs. "What really happened? Why were you trying to sneak in with your hat on?" I look to see if Bunjy has pulled another one of his Ninja stealth moves and crept in quietly behind her. He hasn't yet.

"Nothing. I was just trying to sneak past Bunjy. Not that it worked, I still got a thick lug!" I sink back onto the bed. "Turn the light off, Mom, I've got a headache." My eyelids are heavy with the swelling, and my bulbous forehead is throbbing. With Mongolian idiots swirling in my head, I drift off into a delirious, concussion-induced sleep.

The next day, my parents are too busy to take me to the hospital.

Chip Butties

Smithy and I are walking out of the Wednesbury baths. Famished, we decide to spend our bus fare on penny dips at the rotisserie chicken cafe. We can't afford a sandwich, but for youngsters, Mr. Costas will dip a slice of white bread in the chicken drippings for a penny each.

"Hello, kids. Been swimming, eh? What you want?" Mr. Costas smiles through his big Greek mustache. He is wearing a white kitchen coat, buttoned over his bulging belly.

"Penny dips, please," I say, mesmerized by the chickens slowly turning on the spits.

"How many?"

"We've got sixpence," Smithy answers eagerly.

"Okay, that three each." Mr. Costas dips a thick slice of bread in the sizzling drippings, sprinkles it with salt, and slaps it on a piece of grease-proof paper. He stacks three slices and hands them to Smithy. "Be careful, they hot." He hands me mine and I take a big bite, the chicken grease running down my chin. *Deeelicious!*

"Good, eh!" He smiles, resting his chubby fingers on the metal counter. We leave the sixpence, thank Mr. Costas, and tuck into our hot, greasy bread. "See you next week, kids."

We've gone a mile and have reached Ocker Hill traffic island. As we stand ready to cross, a lorry comes barreling around and drops a big brown bag right in front of us. It slides to a stop at the curb. We watch and wait, but the driver doesn't stop.

"That looks like a bag of spuds!" I exclaim, tearing open the corner for a look. Sure enough, it's a 50-pound bag of King Edwards potatoes. "Give me a hand with this, Smithy."

"No, leave them there. He'll come back."

"He ain't coming back," I insist. "If we don't take 'em, someone else will. Come on, we'll share 'em. Let's get 'em home." Smithy helps me get the bag on my back, and I stagger off toward home, imagining digging into piles of hot chip butties with tea.

"What you got there?" Mr. Willis is standing in front of his shop in his long, brown grocer's coat.

"It's a bag of spuds," I say, struggling to keep going with Smithy balancing the bag on my back. Mr. Willis eyes me suspiciously.

"Where'd you get it?"

"Never mind, it's not yours."

Mr. Willis, who has one bad leg with a jacked-up boot, hobbles to his stock room to check. I keep moving.

Crossing the marl hole, I put the bag down to catch my breath. Smithy attempts to carry the bag, but he can't quite manage it. The thought of piles of steaming golden chips dripping with salt and vinegar pushes me onward. Smithy opens the back door for me and I drop the bag on the kitchen table.

"Where'd you get that?" Mom asks, looking tentatively pleased.

"It fell off the back of a lorry at Ocker Hill island." She looks at me suspiciously. "Ask Smithy, he was with me. Mr. Willis saw me go by with it. Ask him."

"It's true," Smithy corroborates. "He carried it all the way home." Mom inspects the bag and notices the road rash on it.

"Didn't the driver come back?"

"No!" I say. "Finders, keepers. If I hadn't taken it, someone else would have."

"Drag them in the pantry, out of the way," Mom instructs. Smithy helps me move the spuds.

"Let's put your half in these brown carrier bags," I suggest.

"That's okay, you can have them. See you later." Smithy slips out the kitchen door.

"Mom, can we have some chip butties?"

"That's a good idea." She smiles and hands me some of the spuds. "Here, peel these. I'll get the chip pan."

I'm at the sink peeling spuds when Bunjy walks in and sees the enormous bag of potatoes. "Where'd that come from?" he asks.

"It fell off a the back of a lorry and—" Before I can finish, he grabs me by the collar and belts me round the ear.

"Don't smart mouth me!" he roars. "Where'd you get 'em?"

Mom comes in with the chip pan. "Leave him alone! I checked his story with Smithy; he was with him." They launch into a full-blown shouting match, while I go back to peeling spuds. Bunjy finally leaves the room.

"He doesn't believe me, does he?" I ask.

"When people say something has fallen off the back of a lorry, it usually means it was stolen," Mom explains.

I finish peeling the last spud. "Am I still gonna get a chip butty?"

"Of course." She puts the chip pan on the stove. My belly is rumbling as I watch Mom slice the spuds into long, fat-bellied chips. My head still hurts and I'm sore from carrying the bag. Maybe Smithy was right, I should have left the bag where it lay. These chip butties had better be good.

Feeling Spiffy

I'm eleven years old now and starting Willingsworth Secondary School. It is much bigger than Great Bridge and serves lower-income neighborhoods, including families from the Lost City. The Lost City is a 1930s council housing estate that got its name because it is hemmed in by a railway, a canal, and acres of derelict land. It is home to some of the roughest people in Tipton and nobody goes there unless they have to. To get to my new school, I have to walk past St. Marks Church and the Lost City.

It's the first day of school and I'm wearing my new uniform, which was paid for by Social Services. "You've got to be in school by nine o'clock," Mom says. "It's a good walk from here, so be on your way." I wade out through the kids in our kitchen and head up Highfield Road.

I feel spiffy in my new, black blazer, grey shirt, blue- and yellow-striped tie, grey, flannel trousers, and shiny black shoes. It feels good to be dressed the same as everybody else.

I'm passing St. Marks Church and I see a steady stream of kids coming out of the Lost City. Most of them are not wearing school uniforms.

"Oy! Ponce! Who the hell do you think you are?" a tall, scraggly lad shouts in a strong gypsy accent. "Where'd you get them new duds?"

I smile to myself. *Does he realize he's talking to Scruffy McCandless?*

"What are you smiling at?" He comes over and reaches a big, grubby hand for my tie. I smack him up the side of the

112

head and he goes down. *This is a great start.* I continue on my way wondering how this outfit will look by the end of the day.

It's 8:45 and hundreds of us kids are walking up the quarter-mile driveway leading to the school. I see some of my classmates from Great Bridge. "Whoa, Mac!" Robert says. "Hardly recognized you! Even got your tie on." We head toward the main entrance in our matching rookie outfits.

"Hey, lads, here's a bunch of fust-year kids! Look at their pretty uniforms!" an older boy teases. "Grab 'em!"

Five much older lads descend on us. They throw some boys onto the metal roof of the bicycle shed. There are already a dozen kids up there. "Stay up there 'til the bell rings if you know what's good for you!" the biggest bully shouts. "Let's see how many more we can get on the roof before roll call!"

"Quick, this way!" I usher my mates into the main hallway.

"That was close!" Keith sighs, just as a couple of bullies drag him by the collar into the bathroom for the "initiation ceremony." As he's going in, another kid is thrown back out after having his head stuck down the toilet, while it was flushed. "Get me glasses!" he sputters, toilet water dripping from his nose. But he is sucked into the stampede of kids trying to avoid the bullies.

I feel someone yank me back by the collar of my blazer, and I slip out of it. "What the hell?" a brawny lad says. He throws my blazer down and grabs my shirt, ripping off a few buttons. I spin around and kick him in the shins, and he lets go with a yelp. Snatching my blazer, I take off down the hallway. "I'll get you, you little bastard!" he barks, hopping on one leg.

Now, it's time to line up for roll call. I straighten my tie and try to smooth my shirt where the buttons are missing. The boy in line next to me has dripping wet hair. His tie and the top of his blazer are soaked. He turns to me. "I saw what you did. He will get you. I know him; he's from the Lost City." "We'll see," I reply, scanning the crowd.

A clean-shaven teacher with a crew cut and silver-framed glasses steps up to take roll. He looks at the kid next to me. "What happened to you?" Not waiting for an answer, he points to me. "And you, scruffy! Tuck your shirt in and get that blazer on!"

The Falcon

It's a dark, stormy night, with ferocious winds. I'm gazing out the kitchen window at the hutch, hoping my chickens are warm and dry, when I notice a pair of beady, golden eyes looking back at me from the corner of the window. I step out into the pouring rain to investigate. To my surprise, I find a sopping wet falcon with tethers on his feet, huddling on the window sill.

He looks me right in the eyes. I glance down at his fierce claws and think hard about what I should do. I reach for him, thinking he will fly off, but instead he turns toward me. I roll my sleeve down, put my right arm up to him, and he hops on.

I walk back into the kitchen, holding him up on my forearm, dripping wet. His claws grip me, but they do not hurt.

Mom takes one look and shrieks. "What the hell have you got there! Where'd you get that? You and your bloody birds!"

"I just found him on the window sill. It looks like he's exhausted. I can't leave him out in that weather. Look, he's got tethers on his feet. Somebody must have lost him."

"Well, is he safe? What about the kids?"

"He seems to be trained. I think he's just very tired." We decide to put him in the pantry on a pile of rags to dry his feathers.

Later, Mom's making some hot bubble and squeak from leftover dinner. I peek in the pantry and see the falcon has dried out and looks majestic. He gazes calmly over at me. I'm surprised that he doesn't try to fly away. "Shut that bloody door! We don't want him flying out into the kitchen and scaring the kids," Mom scolds.

"He's all right, he's just sitting there. I'm going to give him a bit of my meat." The bird eagerly eats what I give him, preens his feathers, and settles down for the night.

It's Sunday morning and I race downstairs to check on the falcon. Mom has a bacon sandwich ready for me. "Eat this before you do your paper round."

I grab the sandwich and open the pantry door. The falcon looks regal even sitting on a pile of rags. I give him some bacon from my sandwich, which he gobbles down. "Look at him, Mom. He's all dried out and beautiful!"

"Yes, he is, but keep that door closed. The kids are coming down."

I shut the door. "Don't let David or Martin in here. They'll tease him." I grab my canvas newspaper bag and head out the door for my paper round. I ask the news agent if he has an extra round, thinking I will need the additional cash to feed my falcon.

I rush excitedly through the Glebefields, back to the shop to pick up more newspapers, and head on to the Ocker Hill flats. All the while I'm imagining what it might be like if I'm able to keep the falcon.

The newspapers are especially heavy on Sunday, but I feel light on my feet. Around ten o'clock, I stop by the news agent to get my pay and then I run home across the marl hole. I rush in, throw my newspaper bag in the bogey hole, and see Mom sitting quietly in the kitchen.

"What's the matter?" I ask, opening the pantry door. I get my answer when I look inside. "Where's me falcon?"

"Bunjy took him to the pub to try and find out whose bird it is."

I sigh, and close the pantry door, knowing I'll never see my falcon again. "Maybe there's a reward for him."

Mom tries to console me, but I can see in her eyes she's thinking the same thing I am.

The pubs close at two o'clock and I'm looking out the front window for Bunjy. About two-thirty, I see him swaggering across the marl hole, whistling. As I expected, he's had a skinful and the falcon is gone.

I rush out the back door and through the gap in the fence to get away, my head swirling with what I would like to say and do to him. I sit on the grassy bank on the far side of the marl hole and look across at my house. I think of the extra paper round I did this morning and my plans, all for nothing. The magic of the falcon is gone as quickly as it came.

Machete

Bonfire night is in a month. This is a remembrance of the failed Gunpowder Plot to blow up the Houses of Parliament and King James I on November 5th, 1605. Kids make effigies of Guy Fawkes, the most notorious traitor in this plot, who was publicly executed along with some of his co-conspirators. They wheel their dummies around the streets and ask for pennies for the Guy. Passersby give them coins and they use these to buy fireworks. On November 5th, people light bonfires, set off fireworks, and burn the Guy Fawkes effigies.

My mates and I are scouting the marl hole for wood and other objects to burn. We've decided to combine our resources and have one big bonfire in my back yard. To start the pile we've already scavenged some scrap wood and an old armchair from the neighbors.

On the east side of the marl hole, dump trucks have begun to fill in around a row of large, old sycamore trees. "I don't think anyone will care if we cut one of these trees down," I suggest, scouting for the best candidate.

"That's a great idea. Where should we start?" Smithy asks.

"We should probably take out some of the bigger limbs first," I propose.

"Watcha doing?" Alan and his gang materialize behind us.

"W-w-we were thinking about how to get up into this tree to take some branches for our bonfire," I reply.

"Well, how you gonna do that?" Alan pries.

"We're just trying to figure that out," Smithy admits.

"We'll help these kids out," Alan says. "Eric, go get the rope out the back of the car. Maybe we can come to the bonfire."

"You can, if you bring some fireworks," I reply.

"I'll go get my machete," Alan says, striding toward his house.

Within minutes we are gathered at the base of the tree. Alan ties a rock to one end of the rope, and after a few attempts he manages to lob it over a thick bough about 30 feet up. "Now, we need to pull somebody up." He smiles, exposing a rotten tooth. "We're too big, so maybe one of you two."

"What's the plan?" I ask.

"We'll pull one of you up and then you can sit in the tree and start taking the branches off with this machete," Alan says. He ties a big loop on the end of the rope.

"I don't like this idea," Smithy declares.

"Here, I'll do it," I volunteer, feeling a rush of adrenalin as I slip the loop around my chest. "Just lower me down onto the branch below the one the rope's on and I'll cut it off."

"Here, hang onto this." Alan hands me his sharpened machete. It is surprisingly heavy and I think it will do the job nicely. I feel my feet leave the ground as Alan and his buddies hoist me up into the tree.

"Okay, lower me down a little so I can climb onto this branch."

"Right, no problem." Alan grins and they all let go of the rope.

After another one of my Wile E. Coyote moments, I begin free-falling the 30 feet back to the ground, one hand still gripping the rope and the other holding the machete. My feet hit the sloped bank and shoot out from under me, slamming my arse down hard and breaking my tailbone. I slide to a stop 15 feet down the bank and look up to see Alan and his gang howling with laughter. "You okay down there?" Alan guffaws. "That was hilarious. You came down a lot quicker than you went up!"

I jump up, pull the rope off me, and race up the bank toward Alan. "I'll show you funny!" Holding the machete with both hands like a broadsword, I swing wildly at his arms and legs.

"Whoa, whoa! You crazy little bastard!" Alan shrieks. He dances around me like a matador. "Get that machete off him!" he shouts to his mates. "He's gone nuts!"

"You take it off him, he's dangerous!" they yell back, giving me a wide berth and cackling at Alan's antics.

"Stand still and fight, you big yellow bastard!" I challenge. Mad with frustration, I chase Alan out to the street. I stop at the gate and he keeps running.

Smithy catches up to me, looking concerned. "You all right, Tone? I knew we shouldn't have trusted them."

"At least we got a machete out of it," I say, rubbing my aching tailbone.

That was the last time Alan and his gang ever bothered me.

Bunjy Fawkes

It's been a week since the machete incident and Smithy and I have managed to climb one of the sycamore trees and cut off some large branches. Smithy got an old bow saw frame from his brother, and we scraped together enough coins for a new blade. We saw the limbs into 6-foot pieces and manhandle them back to the bonfire. A pile of old wooden crates, furniture, and scrap wood from the neighbors is already stacked on top of the arm chair. Smithy and I are leaning large sycamore logs on the outside of the heap, like a teepee. "This is going to be a massive bonfire." He smiles, wiping the sweat from his brow.

"Yeah, they'll be able to see it for miles," I speculate, adjusting a log that weighs about as much as I do.

It's two weeks 'til November 5th and the bonfire is almost ready. It is about 8 feet high and 8 feet in diameter at the base. It's going to be a whopper of a blaze! I'm in the back yard admiring it in the last few rays of cold, autumn sunlight when Bunjy pulls up on his bike.

"Drag one of them logs into the house, we need some firewood," he demands. "Where's that bow saw you were using?"

"These aren't my logs to take," I protest. "What am I gonna tell my mates?"

"Never mind your mates!" he snaps.

Reluctantly I drag a log into the house, and Bunjy places it across two kitchen chairs. "Now, cut that up into sixteen-inch pieces so it'll fit in the fireplace."

With a lump in my stomach, I begin the treasonous task of cutting up the best of the neighborhood bonfire wood to burn in our fireplace.

Mom sees the sawdust and chunks of wood on the floor. "What's all this mess?!" she shouts. "As if this house isn't small enough, now we have tree trunks in the kitchen!"

"It's free firewood. We'll save on coal money," Bunjy declares.

"What, so you'll have more beer money?" she sneers.

"I'm almost done," I reassure her. "I'll clean this up and put the chairs back." Then I turn around and see Bunjy carrying in another huge log.

"You made short work of that; do this one, too," he insists.

The next day Smithy and Phillip are looking at the now depleted bonfire. "Bloody hell, what happened to our best logs?" Phillip yelps.

"Me dad made me cut 'em up for our house fire," I concede.

"Oh, bollocks to that!" Phillip complains. "We'll have nothing left come bonfire night. Let's move the whole thing somewhere else."

"That's too much work. Leave the bonfire here and I'll fix it," I assure them.

Then, to Bunjy's delight, I spend every spare minute until bonfire night singlehandedly cutting and carrying tree limbs to both feed the house fire and maintain the bonfire stash.

When the big night finally comes, Smithy and I take the standard paper mache´ mask off the Guy Fawkes dummy to paint a Bunjy moustache and sideburns, curly, brown hair, and blue eyes on it. We place it on top of the bonfire with its arms in the air.

"It looks just like him!" Smithy chuckles.

As the bonfire consumes our Bunjy Fawkes, I can't help but look over at my dad. He is glaring right at me.

Mad Axeman

It's a rainy Friday evening and I'm drawing with pencils and charcoal. My art teacher says I should do portraits and develop my shading techniques. I have scoured the Express and Star newspaper and found a small photo of the Avengers (John Steed and Emma Peel); it is one of my favorite TV shows, right up there with Bonanza.

"That's really good," Mom says, looking at my finished drawing. "I like the way you did his bowler hat and umbrella." She places the drawing on the mantel and steps back to admire it.

"I'm going to take it to school on Monday and show it to my art teacher," I say proudly.

The next afternoon I'm in the front yard playing marbles. My dad comes wobbling up on his bike, still in his work clothes. I'm surprised to see him home before the pubs have closed. Reeking of beer, he stumbles off his bike and pushes it against the kitchen wall.

"Oy, where's the big chopper?" he slurs.

"What chopper?" I ask, hoping he doesn't mean my favorite woodcutting axe that I found at the marl hole

"You know which one, that big axe you found. Go get it!"

I bring him the axe.

"Now, find me some string!" I cut him some kite string, which he uses to tie the axe to the crossbar on his bike. He climbs back on, and I'm amazed that he is able to stay upright as he swerves down the side of the house and into the street.

A while later, Smithy and I are sitting on the front wall when Bunjy peddles past us and up the side of the house. I'm not surprised to see that my axe is gone, and I follow him around to the back yard. "Where's me axe?"

"Never mind the bloody axe," he snaps. He drops the bike against the kitchen wall and stumbles into the house.

Hearing the commotion, Mom appears on the step. "Mom, I think Dad sold my axe. He took it with him and now it's gone." We follow him to the front room. Bunjy has hung his coat on the back of the door and is pulling off his boots.

"Where's his axe, you drunken fool? We need that for cutting firewood."

"What have I told you about telling tales?" Bunjy lunges for me, but Mom pushes me out of the way.

"Leave him alone!"

Fuming, he grabs my drawing off the mantel, crumples it, and throws it in the fire. I watch Emma Peel's face burn and turn to ash.

"I'm going to bed. Come on, Joyce," he commands.

"No thanks, go yourself!"

Bunjy storms upstairs and Mom turns to me. "Sorry about your picture. There was no need for that."

"I can draw another picture, but I think me axe has gone the way of the falcon."

"I'll find out if he sold it at the pub and try to get it back." She doesn't look hopeful.

A little later, two burly cops show up at our door.

"Les, there's couple of coppers here for you!" Mom shouts.

Bunjy comes down the stairs in his usual Y-fronts and undershirt, pulling on his trousers. "What do you want?" he gripes. "I'm having me afternoon nap."

"Have you been down to the Railway Tavern in Great Bridge?" the bobby with bushy, ginger eyebrows asks.

"Yeah, I had a few pints after work."

123

"We have a report of aggravated assault with an axe and property damage. Where's your bike?" the taller cop asks, resting a meaty hand on his truncheon.

"Tis 'round the back," Bunjy replies.

"Show it to us."

He leads the policemen to his bicycle. They look at it and then at each other.

"Where's your axe?

"What axe?" Bunjy replies.

"Mr. McCandless, you'll have to come with us." They shove him into the cop car and drive him away, providing fodder for another round of neighborhood gossip.

"What's he done now?" I ask.

"It sounds like the drunken bastard has attacked somebody and smashed furniture at the pub with your axe," Mom says.

A few weeks later, we're sitting in the front room and Mom opens the Express and Star newspaper to an article titled "The Mad Axeman of Tipton." The newspaper vividly describes my father charging into a pub wielding an axe, chasing out a group of customers, and smashing bar stools, tables, and chairs. *Despite numerous witness accounts, Mr. McCandless denied all knowledge of an axe. McCandless avoided more serious charges of assault with a deadly weapon because the axe was never found.*

"Look at this," Mom wails. "The neighbors will love this! It'll be all over the street."

I don't know what to say.

After a while, Bunjy comes home from work. My mom pushes his dinner in front of him and drops the newspaper next to it. "Look at that. You made the paper." He shoves the paper aside and starts on his pork chop.

"What you going to do if them blokes come looking for you?" Mom chides.

"Don't worry, they won't," he insists, wiping his mustache with his sleeve.

"So, what happened to me axe?" I ask from the doorway.

He gives me a hard look. "What axe?" And he turns back to his dinner.

Many years later, I asked him that question again. He told me some gypsies owed him money and wouldn't pay up when he went to collect. When he insisted, they said they had him outnumbered and he'd best walk away. Bunjy walked away and returned to the pub with my axe. When he started smashing the place up, the gypsies gave him his money and scattered. The pub owner called the cops, and Bunjy took off on his bike with the axe. As he crossed the railway bridge on the way home, a cargo train was passing below. He dropped the axe into one of the open cars.

"Gone forever, and the dumb cops never figured it out," Bunjy recounted smugly.

Bad Bananas

I just get back from school and Mom gives me a handwritten list. "Tony, take that over to Mr. Willis."

I cringe. I hate asking for credit with my stammer.

"C-can't anyone else go?"

"No, I want you to go," Mom insists. "The bags will be heavy."

I walk past the crates of cauliflower, cabbage, potatoes, and carrots stacked in front of Mr. Willis's store. The brass bell over the door dings as I step inside and join the line.

Mr. Willis has a new assistant, Lynne Baker, one of our neighbors. I hope that when it's my turn I get Mr. Willis because he knows we need credit and I won't have to explain.

"Next in line, I can help you here." I hand the note to Lynne.

"What's this?" she asks.

"G-g-give that to Mr. W-W-Willis." Lynne looks at me puzzled. "Why? I said I can help you."

More customers pile in behind me. In my head, I'm singing *Just give him the bastard note!* when Mr. Willis notices me struggling and grabs it.

"He's got a stammer," he announces. "You serve the next customer and I'll deal with him." He loads up three bags of food, including 12 pounds of spuds and a big bunch of bananas. He folds Mom's note and slips it under the tray in the cash register, signaling to everyone in the shop that I'm getting the groceries on credit. I grab the bags and hurry out the door, relieved that it's over.

I get home and drop the bags on the kitchen table. "Where's the bananas?" Mom asks. "I'm gonna make banana custard."

I hand her the bananas. "What the bloody hell? These bananas are all bad! Look how brown and bruised they are." She stuffs the offending fruit back into the carrier bag. "Take 'em back! And tell Willis that just because I'm buying on credit don't mean he can give me old food."

"C-c-can't you take them back?"

"No, you're going. That'll teach you to inspect the food when you shop. Get moving, before he closes."

Mr. Willis has already flipped his open sign around to closed when I rush in with the bag of bananas. His two last customers are standing at the counter. "Now what do you want? Wasn't you just in here?"

I hand him the bad bananas. "What's this?" he asks.

"M-M-Mom says these are bad and to b-b-bring them back!"

"Can you believe it?" Mr. Willis complains. "This is what you get for doing somebody a good turn." He examines the bunch. "Tell your mother there's nothing wrong with these bananas. Watch Mr. Willis eat the 'bad bananas'."

We all watch as he peels one of the bruised bananas and eats it, glaring at me. I take a deep breath and shout without a stammer, "Just because we get credit don't mean we have to take bad food!"

A bloke in line looks at me, then at Mr. Willis. "You know, he does have a point."

Exasperated, Mr. Willis slaps a fresh bunch of bananas into a brown paper bag and thrusts it at me. "Here, take these and go. I'm closed!"

I walk back across the marl hole feeling exhilarated. Maybe I don't need to sing the words before I speak. Maybe I just need to get angry.

Flying Jimmy

The Smiths have moved out. Emma Smith, David's mother, says that house has been nothing but bad luck, and losing Colin was the last straw. I miss them all very much. Our new neighbors are the Fellows. The parents, Ted and Anne, have three daughters and a baby son, Jimmy. Mom seems happy that they have younger kids who can play with ours.

I'm in the back yard, throwing bread crusts to my chickens, which are snatching them up and dashing away. I turn and see baby Jimmy next door, in nothing but a diaper, climbing onto the second-story windowsill. Nobody is with him.

"Jimmy! Jimmy! Stay there, stay there!" I drop the bread and sprint toward the gate to Jimmy's yard. He smiles at me, reaches out his arms, and launches himself like Superman off the window sill.

I position myself to catch him, but he hits the clothesline tied to the house and bounces up in the opposite direction. I spin around, backtrack a few steps, and manage to catch him solid in my arms. He has an angry rope burn on his neck and he's howling wildly.

"There, there Jimmy. You're okay now!"

Jimmy's mother, Anne, who is in the kitchen and has heard me shout his name, now hears him screaming. She bursts outside roaring. "What did you do to him?" She slaps me hysterically.

Still holding Jimmy, I turn away from her and take the blows on my shoulders. "N-n-nothing. He j-jumped off the windowsill," I explain.

She yanks him out of my arms. "What do you mean jumped off the windowsill?" She looks at the kitchen window.

"U-u-upstairs. He j-j-jumped out of the bedroom window and hit the clothesline." I point to the open window.

Jimmy's sisters come rushing out to investigate the commotion.

"Jimmy jumped out the bedroom window! You were supposed to be watching him!" Anne rants, dishing out more slaps to the girls.

"It was her turn!" Shelley yelps, rubbing her ear and pointing to her younger sister, Mandy.

"Look at the mark on his neck!" Anne squawks at the girls over Jimmy's wailing. "How am I going to explain that to your father?"

In the chaos, I take the opportunity to slip back across the terrace and into my kitchen. My mother is peeling spuds at the sink. "What's all the row about? Is Anne having a paddy?" Before I can answer, she hands me a knife. "Here, help me with these spuds."

After a few minutes, Anne bursts in holding little Jimmy, who is now resting his head on her shoulder, quietly sucking on his dummy.

"What do you want?" my mother snaps. "Don't be rushing in here!" She wipes her hands on her skirt and moves toward Anne.

Anne looks at me over Mom's shoulder. "I'm sorry, I thought you'd hurt him."

"Hurt who? What the bloody hell is going on?" Mom shouts, getting wild-eyed.

"Little Jimmy jumped out the bedroom window and Tony caught him," Anne explains. "I'm sorry I lashed out."

"Lashed out!" Mom hisses. "Don't you be hitting him. He gets enough of that 'round here!"

I tune out their squabbling and carry on peeling spuds, amazed at how many things in life end in a walloping.

Later, Jimmy's father, Ted, comes home. I hear a lot of yelling next door. Then there is a knock at our kitchen door. Mom answers. It's Ted.

"Hello, Joyce. Is Tony in?"

"Yes, he's right here."

"Thank you, Tony, for catching Jimmy. You know he's my only boy. If he had hit the concrete I would be having a much worse night tonight." He tries to hand me a shiny half-crown coin. "No, no, I don't need that. I'm just glad I was in the back yard when he jumped."

"Well, I want to do something for you." He slips the coin back in his pocket. "You like to fish, don't you? I'm going fishing tomorrow; wanna come with me?"

"I would. Where are you going, Bailey's canal?"

"No, much farther. We're going to Ludlow in Shropshire. You'll have to get up early, though; our first bus leaves at 7:20."

"I'll be ready. How much is the bus fare?"

"Don't worry, I've got it." He smiles. "I'm going to Jean's tackle shop to buy some maggots. You wanna go with me?"

We walk over to the tackle shop and hear someone yell, "Hello, what do you want?" We enter the store, which appears to be empty. I look at Ted, puzzled. Grinning, he points to a birdcage high on a shelf. Ted rings the bell on the counter. "Hello! Can I help you?" the jackdaw responds.

The owner, Jean, appears from the back room, drying her hands with a white towel. "Oh, I see you've met my bird," she says over its raucous monologue. "Quiet down, Jack!" She snaps the towel in Jack's direction. "He'll be quiet now until someone else comes in."

Ted buys four pints of multicolored maggots and a new bait box for me.

Kingfisher

It's 8:30 in the morning and our second bus is crossing an old, stone bridge over the river Severn and pulling up to its final stop in Bewdley. There is a footpath along the river, lined with black-and-white Tudor homes. Their leaded glass windows overlook swans gliding on the gentle current.

"Grab your tackle, let's go. We've got twenty minutes till the next bus." I follow Ted around the corner and am greeted by the smell of fresh-baked bread and sizzling bacon. Ted marches into the Riverside Cafe, drops his gear, and orders two BEST sandwiches and tea. I place my gear next to his and join him in the window seat.

"What's a BEST sandwich?" I ask, my mouth watering.

"Bacon, egg, sausage, and tomato, on crusty bread. You'll like it!" he replies. "Wrap me up a couple of those cheese and onion sandwiches for the road, love," Ted says to the middle-aged woman behind the counter.

I devour my sandwich. Then I sink into my chair to drink my cup of tea and gaze out the window at the quaint buildings and cobblestone streets. The cafe is steamy and warm and Ted and I talk about what we might catch.

After a scenic bus ride through the rolling, sheep-studded Shropshire hills, we arrive in Ludlow. I feel as if I'm stepping into someone else's life as we make our way down cobblestoned streets, past the castle, and through a medieval stone arch to the meandering river. The marl hole seems a million miles away. The morning sunshine glistens on the river Teme, while bright green, sunlit leaves flutter on branches hanging over the water. A gentle breeze carries the scent of cut grass and I hear cows in a nearby field.

We cast our bait, set our rods, and settle down on our fishing baskets. For a while, it's just the two of us. Ted pours me a mug of tea from his flask and hands me a cheese and onion sandwich. "Not too shabby here, is it?" He grins.

An elderly, well-spoken gentleman appears. "Good morning. Lovely day. Any luck yet?" He has faded green, waist-high waders and a tan, floppy hat with multicolored fly lures hooked into it. An antique woven fish basket hangs on a brown leather strap at his side, and he's holding a bamboo fly rod in his hand. He is slight but seems sprightly for his age.

"Good morning!" Ted replies. "No luck yet. We haven't been here long."

His green eyes sparkle. "Not to worry. I have fished this spot for years. You will get fish!" he assures us.

"I'm sure we will. That's a nice rod you have there," Ted remarks.

"Yes, yes! It was my father's. He had it made from split bamboo. This was his reel, too."

The man steps into the weir, walking slowly, scanning the fast-moving water below. He stops about 20 feet in. I watch him cast his line and I admire his seasoned motion and rhythm. Within minutes, his fly rod bends. We watch keenly as he reels in a glistening rainbow trout and soon hooks a second. He stashes them in his basket and makes his way back to us. "Two fish. That will do nicely for supper! Anyway, good luck, tight lines!" And off he goes.

I look over at Ted. "Can you believe that? Two trout in ten minutes!" Just then a bright blue and red kingfisher swoops right in front of us, snaps up a small fish, and lands on the opposite bank.

"Look's like we're being shown how it's done." Ted laughs into his mug.

I get home late Sunday night with six decent brown trout and two eels. Ted caught trout and some grayling, but he always puts the grayling back, because they are such beautiful fish.

Most of the kids have gone to bed and I have the kitchen to myself. As my fish sizzle in butter in the pan, I think back on the peace and beauty of our spot on the river, so far away from the marl hole. I know I will see Ludlow again.

Heads Up

It's a sunny Saturday morning and I've been to Jean's tackle shop to get two pints of colored maggots. I'm getting my fishing tackle together when Mom and Bunjy announce they are going over to the Wagon and Horses pub for a lunchtime drink.

"Tone, the fishing will have to wait a while. Watch the kids till we get back." I put the tub of maggots in the pantry.

I'm responsible for my younger siblings, Sue, Martin, Sheila, Julie, Jean and Paul, who is a toddler. Johnny and David can take care of themselves. Leslie, as usual, is long gone with his mates. To pass the time, I grab the darts my uncle Roger left behind and throw them at the board hanging on the inside of the coal place door. There are many holes in the door outside the perimeter of the dartboard.

The bomb-shaped, brass-barreled darts feel heavy in my hand. They are long, with colorful feathers glued onto wooden stems. I throw the darts a few times but keep having to stop because kids are running in and out, squeezing past the dartboard. Eventually I give up, not wanting to impale anyone. I place the darts on the kitchen table and shut the coal place door.

I get my fishing basket out of the pantry, sit on the kitchen step, and check to make sure that my brothers haven't nabbed any of my tackle. Glancing up at the garden, I see the kids running around in a circle with toddler Paul in the middle. He is picking something up and throwing it in the air, watching it land, and throwing it in the air again. I think he must be playing with a cap bomb until I notice the brightly colored feathers. *Oh shit, Paul's got the darts!*

I dash toward Paul, calling his name. He grabs a dart by the feathers and lobs it into the air. I watch in horror as the heavy dart comes down and plants itself in the top of his skull. Paul looks around on the ground for the dart, unaware that it is stuck in his head like a mini Polynesian headdress.

Hoping to pull it out before any of the kids notice, I run over, grab the dart, and try to yank it out, but it is stuck in the bone. Paul still hasn't figured out what's going on. I grab his head like a rugby ball and pull hard on the dart, which makes him cry.

Johnny and David race over. "If you pull it out, will his brains squirt out?" Johnny inquires. My clandestine operation has been compromised. I remove the dart and I'm surprised to see only a small bump with a little red hole that is not bleeding, even though the dart stuck half an inch into his skull.

I gather the remaining darts. "Don't say anything to Bunjy. I'll tell Mom later." Johnny and David agree to this while inspecting the hole in Paul's head for signs of a brain eruption. Paul stops crying and cheerfully rejoins the other kids, apparently none the worse.

It's been a couple of hours and my parents are back.

"Everything been okay?" Mom asks.

Before I can respond, Johnny blurts out, "Paul had one of Roger's darts stuck in his head!"

"He what?" Bunjy snarls through his beer face. He inspects Paul's head and finds the small bump and hole. "How did he get his mitts on the darts?"

"Tony was chucking 'em at the dartboard and Paul picked them up," David says.

Bunjy moves towards me and I know what's coming next. There will be no fishing for me today.

Another Fine Morning

The next day I'm in the kitchen having tea and toast for breakfast while Mom is boiling diapers. She transfers the hot diapers with her boiler stick onto the washboard, scrubs them, and runs them through the wringer. Mom steps into the pantry to get a block of carbolic soap and shrieks. "There's bloody maggots all over the place in here!"

I dash over and see maggots in various hues of pink, red, yellow, and white, searching every corner of our pantry for food.

"How did they get in here?" Mom grimaces. "You know I hate maggots!"

I see that the lid is off my bait box and it's tipped over. "One of the kids must have opened my bait box."

"What? You put bloody maggots in the pantry with the food?" She has her two-foot-long pine boiler stick in her hand and is using it to shove stuff around on the floor, discovering more and more of the colorful intruders. "How many did you put in here? Don't tell me that quart box was full!" She is getting that wild look in her eyes, and she can tell by the look in mine that it was.

I pick up one of my dad's work boots and pour out a handful of maggots. Mom watches them crawl in and around the lace holes and her face goes white.

Wallop! Wallop! Wallop! goes the boiler stick on my head and shoulders. "Sometimes I think Bunjy's right about you. Get them nasty things out of here! You're not going anywhere until you've picked 'em all up."

I move what items I can out of the pantry and begin picking up maggots. After about an hour, my bait tub is only two-thirds full and they're getting harder to find. For the rest of the day, I come back every half hour and catch a few more stragglers, but I never find where the rest are hiding.

About a week later, I come downstairs for breakfast and watch as Mom opens the pantry door to a squadron of blue bottle flies escaping into the kitchen. "I thought you said you got all the maggots!" She shrieks. "Now we're infested with meat flies!"

Mom reaches for her boiler stick and I run into the back yard. She shouts after me, waving her stick. "I'll see to you later! Go to Willis and get three flypapers. Tell him I'll pay him on Friday."

I don't like asking for credit with my stammer, but it's a better option than another round with her boiler stick.

I return with the flypapers to a scene of mayhem in the kitchen. Mom and my brothers are chasing the flies with rolled up newspapers.

"Keep that middle door closed," Mom shouts. "We don't want them in the other room or upstairs with the baby!" Leslie, Johnny, and David laugh hysterically while smacking giant bluebottle flies and each other.

Mom is much less amused. "Tony, hang one of them in the pantry and shut the door." Mom places a flypaper on the kitchen light and walks into the bathroom to hang the last one.

I do as I'm told, then grab a rolled-up newspaper and start swatting flies.

Bunjy barges in wearing an undershirt and underpants. "What's all the noise about? I was trying to sleep in." He walks into the pantry and immediately backs out with the flypaper wrapped around his head.

"Who put this in here?" he growls, trying to peel off the yellow gooey roll with wriggling flies on it.

"Tony put it in there to catch the flies," Johnny volunteers.

"I should have known it was you, you little idjit! Don't put them where I'm going to be walking," he growls, walloping me on the ear with a sticky hand.

"What, you've just come downstairs and you're walloping him already?" Mom shouts from the bathroom. She walks into the kitchen, "And for Christ's sake, put your bloody trousers on!"

"Did you tell him to hang this in the pantry?" Bunjy barks, struggling to peel the flypaper off his mustache. Mom looks at him and can't help grinning.

The ringing in my sore ear muffles the cacophony of my parents arguing, flies buzzing, and hysterical children smacking everything in sight with rolled-up newspapers. It's another fine morning at 262 Powis Avenue.

Brainwashed

It's spring and we have only a few weeks left of school. Bunjy has injured his back at work and he's home recovering. We're receiving dole money, but it's much less than what Bunjy earns as a furnaceman. Mom still gets a family allowance for each child, and she goes to the post office to collect it every Tuesday. Last week when she went, Bunjy was waiting outside wanting beer money and caused a scene.

Mom has made arrangements so I can pick up the allowance money for her. Today I've already been to the post office, got the money, and paid Willis for last week's groceries. Mom tells me to get coal with the rest.

I'm outside the kitchen door putting newspaper in the bottom of the baby pram so I can fetch the coal in it. The sky is blackening and it's starting to sprinkle. I'm hoping to get the coal home before the downpour.

Dad walks into the kitchen. "Joyce, aren't you going to the post office?"

"Why?"

"I'd like a few shillings for a pint; it helps with the back pain."

"Well, that's a fine excuse for the pint! No, we've no money for beer; you'll have to take your pills instead!" She hands me more newspaper.

"Where are you going with that?" Bunjy asks me.

"He's going to the coal merchant's for half a hundredweight," Mom says. "Leave him alone."

Bunjy eyes me suspiciously and steps outside. "Have you been to the post office for your mother?" He moves toward me. "Give me the money. I'll go get the coal."

Mom steps in. "No! You're not having coal money for beer!"

Bunjy pushes her away and raises his hand to smack her. I jump in and take the blow on the back of my head.

"Leave her alone!" I stand between them, looking Bunjy in the eye.

"It won't be long," Mom shouts over my shoulder. "He's not scared of you. Soon he'll be as big as you are. Then we'll see."

I'm hoping Bunjy won't preempt this and kill me now. I'm grateful he is sober.

"You need to shut up and mind your own business!" Bunjy snaps at me. He marches back into the house, and Mom follows him like a Jack Russell terrier chasing a bull.

"If you want to drink, go see your work cronies and ask them to buy you beer," Mom prods. "You've spent enough of our house money on them."

I rub the knot on the back of my skull and wish she would quit while she's ahead.

"You've got these kids brainwashed against me, especially him," Bunjy complains, pointing at me and stomping into the front room.

My little sister, Jean, is on the sofa, rocking back and forth, and bouncing her head. She has heard my parents yelling and she does this when she gets stressed.

"Stop that bloody bouncing! Now!" Bunjy barks at her. She stops moving and looks up at him in silence.

"What's wrong with that kid?" Bunjy complains. "That's a strange thing for a kid to be doing. Don't tell me I've got another retard like the one with the stammer."

"There's not a thing wrong with any of these kids, especially those two," Mom slings back at him. "If anybody has mental problems in this house, it's you!"

I walk between the contorted faces of my yelling parents and lift Jean off the sofa. Sitting her on my hip, I move toward the kitchen and, hopefully, to safety. I feel her little arms squeeze around my neck, reminding me I have someone else to protect.

Charlie

It's my first time going to the coal yard to fetch coal. I push our baby pram across the marl hole in the drizzling rain, passing my neighbor Ted on his way home from work.

"Where you taking that, in this weather?" he asks.

"I'm trying to get to the coal yard 'fore it closes."

"You'd better shift," Ted says.

The wheels sink into the mud as I shove the pram towards the busy street. I wait at the curb, and an old lady with a brown handbag and a flower-patterned scarf around her head stands next to me.

"Where you going with the pram?" she asks.

"C-c-coal yard."

"Oh! I see." She gives me a toothless smile. "Mind if I hold on as we cross?"

"Of course."

A bloke in a green pickup truck honks as he passes. "Fucking pansy!" he yells. "Where's your handbag?"

Right then I wish we owned a wheelbarrow.

"Take no notice of him, love," the old lady says, shaking her fist at him. "You're a good lad helping your mother."

The light rain becomes a shower as I head down Gilson Street and into the coal yard. I follow the signs to the office and stand on the weigh bridge with my pram. A steel-framed window pops open and I see the grey-haired yard manager looking down at me, winding his pocket watch.

"Left it a bit late, kid." A fire crackles in the potbellied stove behind him, heating a large cast iron teakettle. "Good job Charlie's working over." He leans forward. "What do you want?"

"I w-w-want half a hundredweight," I reply, stuffing my hand in my trouser pocket for the coins.

He slips his watch back into his waistcoat, adjusts its chain, and sticks his fat head out the window to examine the pram. "What? You're gonna put coal in that?" he scoffs. "I don't think that will carry half a hundredweight."

"It will. I've p-p-pushed coal in it before."

"If you say so, kid."

"How much is it?"

"Kibble is ten bob a hundredweight and slack is seven and sixpence."

"G-g-give me half a hundredweight of the s-slack then, please." I hand him two half-crowns, which he puts in his pocket and then gives me change.

"Go over to the canal bank and you'll see Charlie in a barge. Tell him Jack says to load what you need." He shuts and locks the window, then reaches for the teakettle.

I walk toward the canal, but can't see the barge, only piles of coal in a row along the bank. As I get closer I hear the metallic scraping of a shovel and then see pieces of coal fly up onto the bank. I look around the front pile and see a 40-foot long, open-top, steel barge with a man in it swinging a large coal shovel. The rain doesn't seem to bother him.

"Excuse me, are you Ch-Charlie?" The man stands up. Though not a young man, he hops effortlessly out of the barge onto the bank, bringing his coal shovel with him. He's medium height, lean, and muscular. A black, leather waistcoat stretches across his shoulders; it matches his Irish flat cap. His collarless shirt, with the sleeves rolled up past his elbows, is tucked into heavy canvas trousers held up with a brass-buckled army belt. I notice the toes of his heavy boots are worn through, exposing steel toecaps.

"Aye, kid, that's me. Did Jack send you over?" I can see that under the coal dust he is clean-shaven.

"Yes, he d-did. He told me to ask you to load half a hundredweight of slack." I feel bad taking him away from unloading the barge. "Don't you have any help?"

"No, kid, just me. Follow me to the bucket scale." He leads me across the yard to the scale. "Put the buggy in position," he says. "That newspaper you got in there is soaking wet. Here, put one of these old coal sacks in the bottom." Charlie starts to carefully shovel coal into my buggy.

"I normally charge for those sacks, Charlie. Don't be giving them away!" Jack has walked up behind us in his waterproof jacket, a steaming mug of tea in his hand.

"Sorry, guv'nor, my bad. I'll cover it." Charlie tips his hat and continues shoveling.

"Don't be too long over here, Charlie. I need that barge emptied by tonight. I got another coming in early tomorrow." Jack takes a long swig of his tea. "I'll need you to start at six in the morning."

"No problem guv, I'll get it done."

Jack heads toward his cozy den, stops after a few steps, and turns. "He did tell you slack, not kibble?"

"Yes guv, he did," Charlie replies without losing his rhythm. Jack disappears into his office.

"He's g-g-grumpy," I say. "And I wouldn't pay for slack and tell you k-kibble."

"I believe you wouldn't, kid, but some people do." He continues steadily shoveling as the rain runs off the end of his flat cap. "Jack's okay. He gave me this job and keeps me busy. A man needs a job."

When the pram is almost full, Charlie looks around, walks to another pile, loads a big shovel full of kibble, and dumps it in my pram.

"Thanks, Charlie!"

"Say hello to your mom, Joyce, from me. And don't go over the weigh bridge on the way out."

I turn toward the gate and Charlie walks back to the barge, carrying his heavy shovel in one hand like a rolled up magazine.

By the time I get home, the pram has an inch of water in it and I have to transfer the drenched coal into the coal place using a bucket.

"Help him bring the coal in," Mom says to Bunjy. "He's wringing wet with rain."

"He wanted the job, he can finish it," Bunjy snaps, looking up from his newspaper. "Don't forget to bring that pram in the kitchen, dry it, and wipe it down with rags when you're done."

My hands are coated in a soggy coal paste, and sooty water drips across the linoleum floor as I carry the bucket back and forth. It's getting dark and I wonder if Charlie is still digging the coal out of the barge, getting ready for the new load coming in tomorrow. What does he think about when he's shoveling? What's it like to wake up and look forward to a whole day of shoveling coal? My task seems trivial in comparison, and I whip through it with the same steady determination I saw in Charlie.

Very Shiny Coin

I'm twelve years old and Bunjy and Mom have gone to the pub and left me in charge of the kids again. It's raining out, and we're all sitting in the front room around the fire. I'm drawing a picture while the kids are giggling and playing with a mechanical money box someone gave us. The die-cast box is the head and shoulders of a grinning black man with his hand out in front of him. When you place a coin on the outstretched palm and press down, his mouth opens, his arm comes up, and he "eats" the coin.

Martin, who is five, is fascinated and can't stop chuckling. The kids have a handful of pennies and one threepenny bit. After they "feed" them to the man, they empty the box and start over again. I'm just putting the finishing touches on my picture when Sue asks, "Martin, where's the threepenny bit?"

"I ate it," he replies gleefully.

I drop my pencil. "Everybody look for the threepenny bit!"

We scour the bare, wooden floor and it's nowhere to be seen. I empty the money box and find only pennies. It's not looking good.

"Martin, where's the threepenny bit?" He points into his mouth. "I ate it just like the black man." He smiles.

"How do you feel?" I ask, snatching away the money box in case he gets started on the pennies, which are much larger.

"I'm okay."

"Is he going to be all right?" Sue asks.

"Yeah. He'll be fine, but you kids don't say anything to Dad. I'll tell Mom when she gets back."

The children busy themselves playing with popguns and golliwogs while we wait for our parents to return. As soon as they walk in the kitchen, Sue blurts, "We were playing with the money box and Martin ate the threepenny bit!"

"What! Is that true, Tony?" Mom asks.

"Well, we looked all over, but couldn't find it."

"Where were you when this happened?" Bunjy asks.

"It's not his fault," Mom insists. "Don't get started on him. We'll just have to wait until it comes out the other end."

"That's your job, Tony. Go get the chamber pot from under my bed," Bunjy orders. "When he craps, you search through it until you find that coin."

Martin is wildly entertained by the novelty of pooping into a chamber pot, which I then inspect while he looks over my shoulder, snickering. On the third day of poop parsing, I'm overjoyed to find the shiniest threepenny bit coin I have ever seen. I empty the chamber pot and clean the coin.

"Mom, I found it! It looks brand new. Can I keep it?"

"Let me have a look at it. Oh, that is shiny." Mom says, popping it into her purse.

I head outside to get some fresh air and bump into Johnny and David. "Martin told us you found the threepenny bit. I'm going in right now to tell Mom about the sixpence I just swallowed!" David teases.

Old Man River

School's out and Bunjy has arranged for me, Leslie, Johnny, and David to go fruit picking with him. He's still on the dole and found out from his buddies at the pub that you can work for cash picking fruit. He can use what we earn to supplement his dole money and keep some for beer.

It's seven o'clock on a Monday morning and Mom has packed us sandwiches, boiled eggs, and a flask of tea. We are all waiting at the bus stop on Highfield Road. Bunjy is negotiating with a short, muscular bloke in a flat cap for our seats on the bus. The man has a lump of cheese in one hand and a big yellow onion in the other, which he is eating like an apple.

When the old, green, double-decker bus sputters to a stop in front of us, we climb upstairs. Johnny, David, and I share a bench seat and Dad and Leslie get the one behind us.

"So, what are we picking?" Leslie asks.

"Black currants," Bunjy replies, "Five bob a basket."

We roll through Bilston and Wolverhampton and out along the Tettenhall Road into the countryside. After an hour, we pull into a farm and get off the bus. There are at least another 60 laborers, including people from India and troops of gypsies. The Indians are all carrying little plastic buckets. "Everyone who has picked before, stand over here!" the foreman barks. He is a tall, skinny man with bushy sideburns, a flat cap, and shirt sleeves rolled up past his tattoos. "New pickers come with me." He grabs a wooden crate and demonstrates how to pick the currants.

147

"Three things: no leaves in the baskets, no squished fruit, and clean every bush. If you leave fruit, I will have you go back and pick it. If you squish fruit, you're off the field and you can wait for the bus home. I expect you to be at the end of these rows by lunch time."

I can't help thinking of the slave cotton pickers in Louisiana and begin whistling "Old Man River." The foreman eyes me skeptically.

My brothers and I have been picking for three hours now in the sweltering heat. I can't stop thinking of the sandwiches and tea. "Can I have a drink of tea, Dad?"

"Not yet. Let's get to the end of this row."

I notice that the Indians in the next row are sitting on their buckets, which saves their backs and knees. I really wish I had a bucket. My belly is rumbling as I look down the never-ending row. I cram a handful of currants in my mouth just as the foreman roars from a few rows over. "If I catch anybody else eating fruit, you'll be waiting for the bus and not coming back."

The ripe currants burst in my dry mouth. I swallow them, hoping the sweet, refreshing juice doesn't give me the telltale blue mouth. I spend the next hours until lunch devising ways to slip the berries into my mouth and chew them unnoticed by Bunjy or the foreman. In spite of my pilfering, I still manage to fill my baskets.

Bunjy gave each of us our sandwich and boiled egg hours ago. My back and legs are stiff and sore from squatting. I stand up to stretch and see an airplane overhead. The sky is so blue. I wonder where the plane is going and I picture a tropical island surrounded by turquoise waters. I imagine myself lying in a hammock with a cold Vimto in one hand and a chip butty in the other when *Wallop!*

"Stop your daydreaming!" Bunjy snaps. "And get these last crates over to the weigh-in."

148

An Indian family in front of us at the scales hands over their crates. The older of the two farmhands takes one look and dumps the contents onto the ground. "These berries are squashed and full of leaves!" he shouts for everybody in line to hear. "Don't strip the branches. The leaves need to stay on the bush or the bush dies! You're not picking bloody tea leaves, you're picking black currants!" He glares at the family. "One more crate like this and you're back on the bus!"

Exasperated, he turns to his co-worker, "Has anybody showed these jokers how to pick? Go get Bill the foreman to sort these clowns out." He points to a spot away from the scales. "You lot stand over there 'til he gets back!"

During the tirade, everybody else in line is feverishly pulling leaves out of their picked fruit.

"Next!"

The farmhand eyes us kids suspiciously as we hand up our crates. Then he looks pleasantly surprised. "That's more like it. That's what I want to see, nice, clean berries and no leaves." He tallies up our baskets for the day and hands Bunjy the cash.

"Are we going to get any pocket money, Dad?" Johnny asks.

"I'll get you an ice cream on the way home," Bunjy promises, stuffing the notes and coins in his trouser pocket, knowing full well the bus does not make ice cream stops.

Over the next six weeks, we pick sticky black currants, thorny gooseberries, and back-breaking asparagus. We never see a penny of the money, nor do we get even a lick of ice cream.

Windy Miller

After picking fruit all summer, I have never been so happy to get back to school. I'm sitting upstairs on the red double-decker school bus next to my mate Terry amid a tumult of after-school excitement.

Mr. Windmill is on parking lot patrol, making sure no fights break out or teachers' cars get vandalized. He has wooly, brown hair with sideburns and he's wearing a tweed coat with elbow patches over his 6'3", 240-pound frame. He is an unlikely figure to be teaching Shakespeare.

As the bus backs out, my brain switches off and I slide open the top part of the window and shout, "Oi! Windy Miller! Whatcha doing?" The bus echoes with laughter. Mr. Windmill turns around and peers up at me over his glasses, pointing a large index finger.

"He saw you," Terry says, laughing.

The next morning after assembly I'm walking to math class when Keith, a kid from Mr. Windmill's class, approaches. "Tony, Mr. Windmill told everybody that if we see you, have you report to him at the teachers' study. He's not happy."

"Okay, thanks."

"Whatcha gonna do?" Keith asks.

"I'm gonna go see him." I walk upstairs to the teachers' study.

I knock on the door and Mr. Windmill opens it. He has a mug of tea in his hand. "Oh, McCandless! Who sent you here?" He looks over my shoulder.

"Keith Vanes said you wanted to see me."

"Really. Any idea why?"

"I think so."

"It's Mister Windmill to you." He closes the door behind me. "I don't appreciate you shouting out the bus window and calling me names. Why did you do that?"

"I don't know. I just did it."

"Well, you know what I'm going to do now." He reaches for his bamboo switch in the umbrella stand. "Hold out your hand." His huge paw clamps around my wrist and he whacks each of my hands once. Then drops the switch back into the stand.

"Is that it? Can I go now?"

"McCandless, I don't understand you," he says, shaking his head. "Why do you do things like that?"

"I don't know."

"You're better than that. We have hopes for you. You're doing well in class—"

"Can I go now? I'll be late."

Wildcats

I'm in the kitchen making myself tea and toast when I hear a commotion in the back yard. My mother and our next door neighbor, Anne, are screaming at each other. Apparently, my brother David has been teasing Anne's daughter Shelley. Anne yelled at David and Mom jumped in like a banshee.

I walk out the back door to have a look. My mother and Anne are rolling around on the ground in their housedresses, punching each other and pulling each other's hair. They look evenly matched and I wonder who's going to come out on top.

The younger kids are upset by the spectacle. My little sister Julie cries, "Stop them, Tony! Stop them!" I move toward them just as Anne's husband, Ted, rushes through the gate.

"What the bloody hell is going on with you two? You're upsetting the kids!"

Oblivious, Mom and Anne continue like a couple of wildcats. Ted reaches down and grabs Anne, who is still clawing my mother and throwing punches. "Grab your mom," he shouts. "We have to separate them!"

I catch hold of Mom, who is hanging onto Anne's hair with one hand and walloping her head with the other. While Mom and Anne continue screeching at one another, Ted drags Anne through the gate and into their house.

Mom dusts herself off and stomps into the kitchen. Her legs and arms are covered in scratches. "There, there, kids,

152

it's all right. Mom's okay," she reassures them. "David, come here." She cracks him 'round the side of the head. "Don't be teasing them girls next door!"

Twenty minutes later, Ted knocks at the door. I open it and Mom jumps up. "Joyce, it's me, Ted. Are you okay?" Mom bristles. "'Course I am. How's Anne?"

"I'm okay," Anne says over Ted's shoulder. "I'm sorry Joyce, I lost it." Ted watches Mom's reaction.

"Yes, I know. So did I," Mom concedes. "I walloped David. He won't be teasing Shelley again. But come to *me* next time you have a problem with the kids."

"Okay, I will," Anne agrees.

"Come in, I'll put the kettle on."

Ted and I monitor the situation for a while, then decide it's safe to leave them together for now.

Three-Speed Clunker

My friend Colin Wheeldon has a new 10-speed racer bike and wants to ride out to the Coseley swimming baths. Peter Nolan, my uncle Andy's brother, has an old bike he has pieced together from scrapyard bikes. It has cowhorn handlebars and knobbly tires and looks like hell, but it works. I've also been assembling a bike with scrapyard parts, but mine is not finished yet; I still need a back wheel and a chain.

Leslie has somehow managed to get a new, metallic-blue, 5-speed racer bike on credit from Hayles bike shop. It's his pride and joy. Bunjy must have helped him out with the down payment, and Leslie is paying for the bike in weekly installments.

"Hey, Leslie, can I borrow your bike to go to the baths with Colin and Pete?" I ask, hopefully.

"No way. You'll just lose it or break it. I worked hard to get this bike."

"C'mon, Leslie, I'll only be a few hours. You'll be out with your mates anyway."

"I don't think so," he says. He secures the back wheel and frame to the outside kitchen drain spout with a thick-chained, four-barrel combination lock and walks away.

My friends are at their homes waiting for me, and I have no way to contact them. So I sit down, cross-legged, and start fiddling with the lock. After half an hour of trying different combinations, I can't believe my luck when it opens. I wrap the lock around the bike saddle and frame, grab my swimsuit, and head out before my mother sees me.

I blast over to Pete's house in the Lost City. Pete is slim with sleek, light brown hair parted on the side that frames his oversized, blue eyes. I always tell him if he grew his hair longer, he could pass for a girl.

"Wow, Leslie lent you his bike?" Pete asks.

"No. Come on, let's go. Colin will be waiting."

"Tommy said he might come, too. Let's go across the street and ask him."

We wheel our bikes past the tatter's cart parked in front of Tommy's small, terraced house. His father is a full-time rag and bone man, as was his father before him. We walk through the back yard, piled high with treasures deemed too useful to scrap, such as old iron gates, stirrup pumps, wagon wheels, and Victorian chimney pots. Pete knocks on the kitchen door, and Tommy, a brawny, open-faced lad answers.

"Hey, Pete, Tone. Sorry, I can't go swimming. I've got to help me dad." A horse's muzzle appears over his shoulder.

I glance at Pete. "So, I'll catch up with you later," Tommy says. The horse pokes his chestnut head out and eyes us curiously.

"Okay, we'll see you tonight," Pete says as Tommy closes the door.

"They keep their horse in the bastard kitchen?" I ask.

"Yeah, they do that sometimes."

"Must get a bit crowded in there when it's time to make dinner."

"Oh, they've put him out by then," Pete says, climbing on his bike.

I speed along on Leslie's bike, periodically slowing down to let Pete catch up on his old 3-speed clunker. We pick up Colin on his new, golden 10-speed bike. It's even fancier than my brother's.

We arrive at the baths, and I use Leslie's combination lock and chain to secure all three bikes to the racks. Pete's old bike is in the middle. "There, the bikes are safe. Let's get swimming. I can't stay too long because I need to get this bike back before Leslie gets home."

After a couple of hours, Colin and I are teasing Pete and chasing him out of the pool cafeteria. He disappears around the corner to the bike racks and then reappears, laughing so hard he falls onto his back on the grass.

"What's so funny?" I ask, catching up with him.

"They've stole your bikes! There gone!" he chortles, barely able to breathe. "They left my old beater here and just took the valves out of my tires."

"That's not funny, Pete."

"You might not think it's funny, Tone, but it's true," he howls. Colin and I look at each other and then back at Pete, who is grabbing his knees and gulping for air.

Still holding out hope, I round the corner and gasp at the sight. Pete's bike is there, with flat tires, and the severed chain hanging loose through the back wheel. "Oh shit!" I shout. A knot tightens in my stomach and a tidal wave of remorse makes the hair stand up on the back of my neck. *Leslie will never forgive me for this.*

We report the theft to the manager of the swimming baths and then hurry to the local police station to fill out a report. No one is hopeful about getting our bikes back.

Finally we walk back to Colin's house, with Pete pushing his bike and sporadically bursting into fits of laughter. Surprisingly, Colin's father takes the news calmly. "Well, that's bad luck. But sometimes stolen bikes do get returned."

I listen to him, knowing that my homecoming will not be like this. Reading the expression on my face, Colin's father asks, "Do you want me to go with you to tell your parents what happened?"

"No, thanks. I'll be okay." I turn away and begin the longest walk home of my life.

Big Uggy

I'm thirteen years old and my dad, Leslie, and I are visiting my father's family in Coleraine, Northern Ireland. My grandparents are divorced now, and we're staying with my grandmother in her terraced house on a hillside overlooking the river Bann. The area is nicknamed Wuthering Heights.

It's Saturday morning and we're having a cup of tea with Grandma. "You's boys have grown since I last saw you!" She smiles. "And Tony, you've fixed your stammer."

"Sometimes," I answer, looking away.

My Aunt Jean pulls up in her Ford Cortina to take us all to the Yellow Man seaside festival at Port Rush. She is a lovely, kind woman and I'm looking forward to spending the day with her.

It is sunny and warm at the festival and the grownups buy us packets of salty, dulce seaweed and bags of rich, buttery Yellow Man rock candy. With our faces and hands sticky from the treats, we make our way to the shore.

Grandma and Aunt Jean sit down to chat and my brother and I join some kids who are jumping off the rocks into the swimming hole. It's about a 15-foot drop. I dive off without hesitating and climb back up. The other kids are surprised. "Where are you from?" the biggest lad asks.

"England. I'm over visiting family."

"You should try the next spot up," a tall, red-haired boy with freckles suggests. He points to a ledge another 10 feet up.

"Let's go look," I propose, and we all clamber up.

"English, this is where we dive off," the oldest lad says, doing his best to look sincere.

"Show me, then," I challenge. The boys back up, pushing each other to the front.

"Let's see you do it and I'll follow," a spunky, raggedy-haired kid pipes up.

"All right, you paddies, move out the way." I look over the edge at the sparkling teal-colored water 25 feet below, and without another thought, I dive off. It is a long way down and I don't care. Within seconds, I break the water and my hands hit the golden sand 20 feet beneath the surface.

I feel weightless in amongst the sunbeams piercing the clear water. I swim over to a long piece of seaweed and yank it out, picturing myself whipping my brother Leslie with it. I hover over the sand for a few more peaceful moments before swimming along the bottom to the other side to sneak up on him.

The moment I surface, someone grabs me by the hair, yanks me out of the water, and wallops me while I try to catch my first breath. "You idjit! Showing off, again!" my father roars. "Ye nearly give your grandmother a heart attack. You've been down there a long time, what was ya thinking?" His eyes look as though they're going to pop out of his head.

"I was getting this," I say, showing him the seaweed. He yanks it out of my hand and smacks me on the head with the bulbous end. As he's pounding me I can't help wondering what the neighborhood boys who nicknamed him "Big Uggy," after a cartoon cave man, would say about this.

"Les! Les!" my grandmother shouts. "What are you doing?" Bunjy stops midswing, throws the bruised seaweed to the ground, and rushes over to her.

The Irish boys gather around me. "Was that your da?" the raggedy-haired kid asks.

"Yes," I say, rubbing my head. I bend down and pick up my seaweed.

"Why did he wallop ya?"

"He thought you tricked me into jumping off. Why didn't you jump in after me? That would have helped."

Bunjy sees the crowd of kids around me and barks, "You stay off those rocks!"

"Your dad's a nutter!" the spunky boy volunteers.

"I know."

Full of adrenaline from the dive and the beating, I practice cracking the seaweed like a whip, imagining myself as Rowdy Yates from Rawhide. My new friends are enjoying the spectacle. "Hey, let me have a go!" the oldest boy asks. I'm stepping toward him to hand him the seaweed when the whole group scatters like a herd of startled deer.

"Look out, he's coming back!" one of the boys warns.

Before I can turn around, Bunjy grabs my shoulder. "The reason I walloped you is them local kids knew it was too shallow and they talked you into diving off like an idjit."

"I knew it wasn't too shallow," I reply. "I'd been in already." Bunjy is snarling at my "backchat" when Aunt Jean, jumps in.

"Leave him alone, Les. Let's go get something to eat." Bunjy lets me go, but not before he yanks the seaweed out of my hand and tosses it back in the water.

Jean looks at me and I see the sadness in her eyes. "Your dad's got a lot on his mind, Tony, and you really scared Mother."

I nod silently, hoping the explanation makes her feel better. It's certainly not helping the lumps on my head.

Broken-In Shoes

It's a warm Saturday afternoon and my friends and I are swimming in the lake on the private sanatorium hospital grounds. The occasional puffy, white cloud looks out of place against the bright summer sky. We run and dive off the bank and swim out into the deep, cool water, looking for the raft someone has made out of planks tied onto empty 50-gallon plastic drums.

We find it at the end of the lake near the bullrushes and sycamore trees. Mick and I push it back toward the bank. The raft is 8 by10 feet and has a smooth deck.

I pull myself up onto it and then dive straight down as far as I can with my eyes open. At about 25 feet it gets dark and cold and my ears start to hurt. I look up and see the raft, surrounded by green light and pairs of feet dangling in the water. I float peacefully for a few moments wishing I could stay down longer, and then swim back to the surface.

After a few hours of swimming, Mick complains, "Bloody hell, I'm starving. Let's head home and get some grub." We dive off the raft and swim back to shore to dry off and get dressed. I put on my new Clarks Wayfarer shoes. They're brown leather brogues and the soles have animal tracks on them. Inside the heel is a magnetic compass. It was my turn to get a new pair of shoes and I picked these out specially.

The other boys take off and Mick and I walk along the lake until we reach a concrete panel fence with a barbed wire top. Some of the panels are broken. "This is a grocery store

160

warehouse," Mick says, looking through a hole in the fence. "Let's see if one of the vans is open. Maybe we can grab some biscuits."

"Wait a minute. That's not good," I say looking around at the empty facility.

"Come on, the place is empty." I wait and watch while Mick scopes things out. He checks out the trucks, but they're all locked. "Come on," he calls. "There's nobody here!" He climbs onto a van, then a big lorry, and jumps up onto the roof of the building. I follow him tentatively.

From the roof, we can see out over the shimmering green lake and into the windows of some of the neighboring homes. We walk to the other side and look down on another parking lot with more vans. Then suddenly, with wild abandon, we chase each other up and down the peaks on the roof, forgetting all about our rumbling stomachs.

After a while we sit down to rest. As my breath gets quieter, I hear the crackle of a walkie-talkie. I peek over the edge of the roof to see a bobby directly beneath us.

"I'm on the north side," he says. "You go 'round the south side." I see his police car parked back at the entrance to the parking lot.

Mick is right behind me. "Coppers!" I whisper. We rush to the opposite side of the building to sneak down. Mick hangs off the side of the roof and drops onto the top of a lorry. His landing is fairly quiet, but then he sprints across it, *boom, boom, boom*, drops onto the cab, and slides to the ground. He heads toward a hole in the fence.

The thunder of his footsteps is still echoing and I realize I have only seconds to escape. I jump onto the top of the lorry, landing with an enormous bang. *Oh shit!* In a panic, I run and leap off the lorry roof, 15 feet up, and hit the concrete on my hands and feet like a chimp. The momentum flips my feet over my head, sending my shoes soaring and slamming me flat on my back.

My right foot throbs as I listen for the sound of approaching police, convinced I'm caught.

Mick pokes his head back through the fence. "Come on, hurry up!" he urges. "There's nobody coming yet!"

I limp over to my shoes to find that the impact has ripped the rear seam of each shoe from top to bottom. I wonder how I will explain this as I schottische my way to the fence and dive through the hole.

"What'sa matter with your foot?" Mick asks.

"Never mind me foot, look at me bastard shoes!" I say in horror. The back of each is torn open in a "V" and they won't stay on my feet.

Mick peers back through the fence. "Bollocks to your shoes. We've got to go!" I roll the shoes and swim shorts in my towel and hobble after him, trying to run on the underbrush and twigs in my socks. "Come on," he says. I'll give you a piggy-back."

I jump on and Mick struggles, crashing through the woods with me hanging on and looking over my shoulder. "Stop, Mick. I'm too heavy for you. Good try, though."

He lets me down and we sit while he catches his breath. "Let's get to the side of the lake and pretend we're just hanging out," he pants.

"No, that ain't gonna work. How am I going to explain my blown-out shoes and my limp? Let's just keep going."

For the next 10 minutes we wind our way through the woods and pop out through the fence near the canal railway bridge, 200 yards from the main road. I hobble painfully on the gravel. "Let's split up. They're looking for two kids. You follow the canal and I'll take the road."

Mick gives me a nod and takes off running along the canal tow path.

After I've gone about a mile, I reach the Lost City where the tatters and gypsies live. "Oi, McCandless, what's going on?" some ragged kids yell. "Why are you walking in your socks? What's wrong with your foot, pegleg?" they tease, throwing pebbles at me. "Can't you afford shoes at your house?"

A pebble bounces off my head. "Fuck off!" I shout, realizing I'll be in trouble if they start a fight. Miraculously, neither the cops nor the Lost City scrappers manage to get hold of me. I hobble the rest of the way home in my socks, getting strange and concerned looks from passersby.

It's eight o'clock at night when I slip on my busted shoes outside our house. My right foot barely squeezes in and the heels slap the floor as I try to walk inside and navigate through the kids running around the kitchen and front room.

"You're late. Where you been?" Mom asks.

"Swimming," I say, keeping my feet pointed in her direction. Little Paul wanders over and I push him in front of me to keep him from spotting the backs of my shoes. To my relief, Bunjy is not home.

I slip upstairs, place my shoes under the bed, toes pointing out, and go back down for some tea. I try not to limp while keeping my sore foot out of the way of the kids romping around the kitchen.

The warm steam from the tea dampens my nose as I hold the cup in front of my face and contemplate the possibilities. My mom's voice brings me back. "We're gonna watch Rawhide on the telly. I know you like that," she says. "I've put two shillings in the meter, so it should last for the show."

"That's all right, Mom. I'm going to bed." I do my best to walk normally out of the room. I'm worn out from the long journey home and as I gingerly pull myself up the stairs I try not to think too much about tomorrow and having to explain all of this to Bunjy. I flop into bed and drift off into a deep, troubled sleep.

It's 6:30 on Sunday morning and I have to get up for my paper round. Forgetting about my foot, I hastily swing my legs out of bed and stand up. Racked with pain, I fall back onto the bed. My right foot has a 3-inch-wide bruise all the way around it and is badly swollen. My toes look like little, purple potatoes and I can't move them.

I limp down to the kitchen. Mom is already up, making a bacon sandwich for me to take on my round. "Here's some tea and toast. Why are you limping?" She looks down at my foot. "What's the matter with your foot?"

"I think it's broken. I can't move my toes."

"How the hell did you do that?"

"I was climbing on a van yesterday and I jumped off."

"What van? Where? Any coppers involved?" she says with her eyebrows gravitating toward one another. "We don't need coppers coming to the house."

"There weren't any coppers." I blink.

Mom inspects my foot. "Ah, that looks broke. We'll have to go up to the Dudley Guest Hospital and have it x-rayed. Grab your shoes and coat; let's get the next bus."

"I've got a problem with my shoes."

"Now what?" She props her hands on her hips. "You've got new shoes. Where are they?"

"They're under the bed, my side." I cringe.

Mom quietly goes upstairs, returns with the shoes, and pulls out my shredded wool school socks. Then she spots the split seams on the backs of the shoes.

"These shoes are ruined!" she yelps. "I ain't even finished paying for them yet! And what happened to the socks?"

"Well, I walked home from the Sana lake in them."

"You walked three miles with a broken foot in your socks?"

"Well, my shoes wouldn't stay on."

"Oh, bloody hell. What about your paper round?" She purses her lips. "Mr. Davies is going to be pissed. And we'd better hide these socks." She throws them under the sink. "We don't want Bunjy to see them."

164

The smell of the bacon has roused my father and we can hear him moving around upstairs. "What we gonna tell him about your foot and the shoes?" Mom whispers.

"Tell him I fell out of the tree again."

"Well, that ain't gonna make him too happy. He told you not to climb trees anymore." Bunjy barges into the kitchen. "What trees?" He looks at Mom, who is holding my blown-out shoes. "Are those his new shoes?" he growls, snatching one out of her hand and inspecting the ripped seam.

"They're both like that," Mom reveals. Bunjy's eyes narrow as he reaches for the other shoe.

"You bloody idjit! You've ruined your new shoes!" He wallops the top of my head with one shoe, then grabs me by the arm, but Mom jumps in. "Hold it! He's got a broken foot, too."

"What?" he barks. "How'd he do that?"

"You better ask him."

Bunjy shoves me away and I stumble onto my broken foot. "Well, what did you do?"

"I was climbing a tree on the marl hole to get firewood and the branch broke. I landed on the sloping bank and it busted me shoes."

Bunjy glares at me. "How high were you in that tree to fall and bust two shoes?" He steps forward and smacks me again. "What did you really do? Any cops involved?"

"I told you what happened." I brace myself on the kitchen sink and wonder how far this will go.

"Okay, that's enough," Mom shouts. "Remember his foot. You'll need to take him up to the hospital."

"I ain't taking him to the hospital. What's he gonna wear on his feet to get there?"

"Well, I can't take him," Mom snaps. "I have kids to feed."

"Then he'll have to wait," Bunjy snarls. He tromps into the bathroom for a loud piss. "I hope you have some of that bacon for me." The toilet flushes. "What about his paper round? The idjit's gonna get fired!"

"If you ain't gonna take him, maybe you could walk over and tell Mr. Davies he's broke his foot," Mom suggests.

"I ain't going over there, I've got things to do."

"Like what? What things you got to do on a Sunday morning except get ready for the pub?" Mom puts my bacon sandwich and a cup of tea on the table. I hobble over, giving Bunjy a wide berth.

Later that day I'm on the bus with Mom heading to the hospital. I'm wearing one of Leslie's old shoes on my good foot and one of Bunjy's old work socks on the other. Mom is quietly counting the change in her purse for the fare back home, and I feel bad that I'm putting her through this.

All the toes on my right foot are broken except the big one, and I have a boot cast up to my knee. My purple toes stick out the bottom, looking like grapes on a skewer. I'm slow on the crutches when we leave the hospital. "Let's try to cross here without getting mowed down," Mom shouts over the roar of traffic. She hangs onto my sleeve and we make our way across four lanes to the bus stop.

We wait at the bus stop and Mom asks anxiously, "What about school?" She shakes her head. "Bunjy is gonna love this."

I put my arm around her shoulder. "I'm sorry for all the trouble."

She forces a smile. "Don't you worry, we'll work this out. I'll go see Mr. Davies when we get back, and in the morning I'll go to your school. Now, how are you doing on those crutches?"

I stand up and pivot on the crutches. Then I swing one like a broadsword and grin. "These crutches might come in handy."

"Don't even think about it," she says. "Come on, the bus is here."

When we get home Bunjy is in the front room. I stay in the kitchen while Mom gives him the news. "He's on crutches; he's got four broken toes and a boot cast. He'll need to go back in three weeks to get his foot looked at."

"Idjit! You mean he's going to be stuck around the house with me for three weeks?"

"No, he wants to go to school."

"Good. But how's the clown gonna get there and what's he gonna wear for shoes?"

"I'll polish up one of Leslie's old shoes, and I'll go down to the school tomorrow to see what I can sort out."

It's Tuesday morning and there is a cab Social Services has arranged waiting outside our house. It's a big, black Austin Cambridge with smooth, leather seats. I've never been in a fancy car like this before and I can't wait to ride in it.

The driver looks tidy with his short, black hair, sideburns, and pressed white shirt. He owns the Cottage Spring pub and he knows my dad well; Bunjy's one of his best customers.

"Good morning. My name's Jim. I'll be your driver for the next three weeks." He opens the car door and I climb in the back seat. He places the crutches next to me. "How'd you do that, son?"

I tell him the same story I told Bunjy, guessing they'll probably discuss it later at the pub.

"You're lucky you didn't break your bloody neck!" He gets in the driver's seat. "Willingsworth school, isn't it?"

"Yes, please. That'll do."

"Do you want the radio on?"

"Yeah, put the Radio One morning show on." I run my hand over the smooth leather seat.

We drive through the school gates toward the main building. The Austin has no taxi sign and the kids are wondering who the posh visitor in the shiny, black car could be. The driver slows and honks at a herd of kids blocking the driveway. They part like sheep and try to catch a glimpse through the windows.

I spot my mates Terry, Colin, and Mick, and I roll down the window. "Oi! Peasants!" I shout.

"What the hell? It's McCandless!"

I give them a royal wave as we roll past.

"Pull over! Pull over!" they yell.

"No, can't do that," Jim says. "Close the window."

He pulls around to the front office, gets out of the car, and opens the door for me. I thank him and as he hands me my crutches, I notice some girls are watching me. Then my old nemeses, Lee and Alan, see me. "Oi, Scruffy! What did you do, win the football pool?"

I smile to myself. *If you only knew!*

The Tie

I'm finally off my crutches, and we're filing into the main hall for assembly. Headmaster Benjamin Bailey is up in his pulpit. All the kids refer to him as Benji. He's in his sixties, old school, and with his shiny, bald head and big ears, he looks like Yul Brynner's big brother. Benji's large frame is draped in a long, black cape. I call it his bat cape.

Mr. Williams, the deputy headmaster, is on door duty. He's a tall, imposing man with thick, grey hair and large, metal-framed glasses. His posture and speech are like that of a British army officer. He teaches English and he's appalled by our, as he calls it, "working class dialect." God knows how he ended up in Tipton.

As I approach the door, Mr. Williams grabs me by the ear and yanks me out of line. "Where's your tie, McCandless? How many times do I have to tell you to wear your tie?"

I bat his hand off my ear. "My tie? Look at all these other kids without ties. Why do you single me out?"

"Never mind the others. Most of them are a lost cause."

"I'm no different to any of these."

He pushes me back in line. "Come to my office after assembly."

Half an hour later I knock on Mr. Williams's door. He calls me in and steps out from behind his desk. "McCandless, why don't you wear your school uniform?"

"I do, except for the tie."

"The tie is part of your uniform," he insists, looking down at me. "I've been looking over your grades. You're doing very well in your classes. You could go to college, make something of yourself—"

"Is that all, sir? I'm late for class."

The Good News

It's recess and Pete and I are milling around. "You see that girl over there?" Pete says.

"Which one?"

He points. "The one with the long hair and the big tits."

"Oh, now I do. She's cute." We watch her laugh and joke with her friends. "What about her?"

"I'd like to take her to the youth club tonight." He gazes at her and sweeps the hair off his face.

"Why are you telling *me?* Go ask her, then."

"I can't ask her." He shoves his hands in his pockets and looks down at his feet. "I've been trying to get up the courage for weeks."

"Do you want me to go ask her for you?"

"Yeah," he says, looking relieved. "I'll wait here."

"What's her name?"

"Christine."

I stride over to Christine and her friends, who stop talking and look at me cautiously. I step in front of Christine and ask, "You're Christine?"

"Yes, why?" she replies with a cheeky grin. "I see that your foot is better."

"My friend Pete, standing over there…" I point at Pete, who looks away, embarrassed. "He wants to take you to the youth club tonight. And he wants to know if you want to be his girlfriend."

She strokes her chin and looks over at him. "Yeah, I know Pete. Tell him no." She smiles. "But you can take me."

"What?" In shock, I agonize over the moral dilemma for at least ten seconds, then reply, "Okay, I'll meet you here at seven o'clock."

"Okay," Christine says, amidst a chorus of giggles from her friends.

Beaming, I saunter back to Pete, He's rubbing his hands together with a big smile on his face. "Well, it looks like that went well."

"It did," I say. "Do you want the good news or the bad news?"

"Give me the bad news first."

"She said no."

Pete's smile fades. "And you say there's good news?"

"Well, she says she'll go with me."

"You bastard! That's *my* girl. I've been chasing her for weeks!"

"I told you you should have asked her yourself."

"Are you going?"

"I was going anyway."

"Bastard!"

I walk back to class with a crestfallen Pete, while I let it gradually sink in that "Scruffy" got the girl.

If the Shoe Fits

I'm sitting in French class waiting for the teacher, Mr. Roberts, who is 10 minutes late. The class is starting to get a bit raucous and is unaware that Mr. Williams, the deputy headmaster, is teaching the class next door.

Suddenly the door connecting the adjacent classrooms bursts open and Mr. Williams charges in and slams his bamboo cane twice on the nearest desk. "What's all this noise?"

The room immediately falls silent. "Get your books out and read *quietly* while I find Mr. Roberts." He shakes his cane at us.

Mr. Williams steps into the hallway, closing the door behind him. Stunned, everyone is quiet for a few minutes, but soon things deteriorate to the usual level of adolescent chaos in the absence of supervision. I watch Keith and Robert throw gym shoes at each other. One shoe bounces off the wall and lands on my desk

"Hey, quit that!" I grab it to hand it back to them just as Mr. Williams bursts in.

"McCandless! I saw that!" I look down at the shoe in my hand and then over to Keith and Robert.

"Step out front," he orders. I stand in front of him. "There are rules about throwing things in class! Give us your hand."

"He didn't throw it," my mate Terry interjects.

"Be quiet, Pierce. I saw the shoe in his hand." *Crack! Crack!* Mr. Williams smacks both my open palms with his

172

bamboo cane. "Report for detention tonight. Now sit down, McCandless. Let that be a lesson to you all."

Take Your Lumps

It's 8:50 in the morning and I'm standing at the back of the school gym with the smokers so my buddy Terry can have a cigarette.

"Whatcha got?" Anthony Whitney asks.

Terry's cousin, Percy, has a pack of John Player No.6. Percy dangles a cigarette in front of Anthony. "Well, are you going to class?"

"Yeah, yeah, whatever." Anthony snatches the cigarette and lights it off Percy's fag. "Actually, no, probably not."

"Dammit, why don't you just go and get your licks? Are you going to play trotter for the rest of the school year?" Percy prods through a puff of smoke.

"Maybe. But I ain't having six whacks of Benji's cane today," Anthony says, getting interrupted by the first bell.

The lookout kid on the corner shouts, "Williams is coming!" Everyone puts out their cigarettes and hides their packs. Anthony jams his fag in his mouth and sprints halfway across the tennis courts. Looking back over his shoulder he shouts, "Come on, Wilkie, let's go!"

His buddy, a swarthy lad with early sideburns, shrugs and follows him. They squeeze through a hole in the tennis court fence and head toward the railway bank.

"You clowns!" Percy shouts. "Don't do it! Take your lumps!"

It's almost noon and I'm in metalwork class. Looking out the window, I spot Wilkie climbing through the wire fence between the railway bank and the playground. "Hey, it looks like Wilkie hurt his foot," I say. Terry and I watch as he hurriedly hobbles across the playground and out of sight.

Terry looks puzzled, "Where do you think he's going? And where's Whitney?"

It's been about ten minutes and now Headmaster Bailey is climbing through the railway fence in his long black cape. "It looks like Benji's had enough for today. He's playing truant, too!" I quip as the other students gather for a look.

"Hey, what's going on?" Mr. Mills, the shop teacher asks. "Get back to your workbenches."

"Look, Benji's playing trotter!" I announce.

"That's *Mr. Bailey* to you, McCandless!" Mr. Mills reminds me. Puzzled, he gazes out the window. We all go back to our benches and Mr. Mills slips out to investigate.

"Hey, Benji's coming back for his lunch!" Keith shouts. We all rush to the window and watch the headmaster make his way back down the railway bank. Within minutes, two police cars are parked up by the railway fence and four uniformed bobbies rush down the track. They return carrying heavy, black trash bags, which they place in the trunks of their cars. Then they get fresh bags and head back down the track.

The lunch bell rings and we all surge into the schoolyard. I make a beeline for the dining hall and notice a girl from the senior class sobbing hysterically. "What's the matter?" I ask, walking up to her. She lets out an ear-piercing scream and attacks me like a banshee, punching me, scratching and kicking. I block her blows, trying not to hurt her, and in the end I grab her wrists.

Her two friends push me away, and try to comfort her. "Don't you know who this is?" one of them shouts. "This is

Anthony Whitney's girlfriend! He's been killed on the railway."

"What?" I realize I've been watching the cops carry pieces of Anthony's body in the black bags. Two teachers approach us, and Mrs. Mills leads Anthony's girlfriend to the office. The other teacher, Mr. Guest, glares at me.

"Fighting with girls now, are we? What did you say to her?"

"Nothing. I just asked her what was wrong and she went off."

"Oh, really. Come with me to the office."

"No, really, that's what happened," my mate Pete says. "I was with him. She attacked him."

Mr. Guest ignores Pete and leads me to Benji's office. We walk past Wilkie getting his foot bandaged and Benjy talking to the cops. "Wait there," Mr. Guest barks.

I sit down in the hall and think of times when my mates and I have run and jumped on a slow freight train to catch a free ride. Anthony and Wilkie must have been doing the same when Anthony fell under the train and Wilkie hurt his foot.

"We're still completing the search," one policeman says. "The body is spread out quite a ways along the track."

I remember my last glimpse of Anthony Whitney, laughing and slipping through the fence. I try to wrap my brain around the idea that he died because he didn't want to get his hand caned by the headmaster and how this can never be reversed.

Me, I'll just take my lumps.

Benji spots me. "What's he doing up here? Get him out!"

"Go get your lunch." Mr. Guest snaps. "We'll deal with you later!"

Piss and Wind

I'm in geography class, sitting in the front row. Our teacher, Mr. Brown, is an athletic young man who comes to school on a ten-speed racer bike. All the girls think he's cute. He's writing on the chalkboard when Deputy Headmaster Williams walks in and has a quiet word with him. Mr. Brown sits down at his desk while Mr. Williams brings in an older boy. I recognize him as one of the Lost City gang.

This should be interesting.

Mr. Williams pulls him to the front of the class by his shirt sleeve and orders him to stand still. "Now, class, this is a prime example of how not to behave and how not to dress for school." He points at the boy's clothes with a wooden yardstick. "As you can see, this hooligan is wearing short sleeves, jeans, and no coat or tie. I caught him fighting in the hallway."

"I wasn't fighting," the boy insists. "I was defending myself." He glares defiantly at Mr. Williams.

"Be quiet, Paskin," the deputy headmaster orders, looking down at the boy. "As you can see, open-neck shirt and no tie." He whacks him on the chest with his ruler, and I think of all the times Mr. Williams has pulled me up for no tie.

Paskin slaps the ruler away. "Don't do that. There's nothing wrong with the shirt, it's a Ben Sherman."

"I told you to be quiet," Williams snaps. "Ben Sherman? Isn't that skinhead attire?" he scoffs. "That probably explains the big, laced-up boots."

176

"Those are Doc Martins. And polished up smart," Paskin adds with a smirk.

"What I have a problem with is the shaved head." Mr. Williams bops him on the head with his ruler. "We'll have no skinheads in our establishment!" Paskin slaps the ruler away again. Mr. Williams grabs his arm and tries to bat him some more. Paskin finally loses it, and a full scale fistfight breaks out. We watch in stunned silence as he pounds Deputy Headmaster Williams.

Mr. Brown jumps in between them. "Stay out of it!" Paskin shouts. "He's got it coming." I'm in full agreement.

"You're in enough trouble," Mr. Brown says. "Calm down and leave. Now!" He pushes Paskin away, hoping he is not in for a clobbering, too.

Paskin pauses. "You're right. The old bastard's not worth it." He turns to the class with both fists in the air, posing like the Hulk. "See, he's all piss and wind," he roars. "See you later, kids!" He grins and stomps out of the room.

"Don't bother coming back," Mr. Williams yells after him. "You're expelled!"

Mr. Brown leads the deputy headmaster to the nurse's office, and the class erupts in laughter and commentary. The girls are swooning over Mr. Brown's heroism. I sit at my desk, smiling. *Mr. Williams picked on the wrong guy today*

Hooligan

Lunchtime is over and Terry and I are walking into woodworking class. We head straight to our workbench at the back of the room. Our teacher, Mr. Woodward, comes in carrying a large box and kicks the door shut behind him.

There is a loud, prolonged clatter to my right and I look down to see a big pile of freshly glued, wooden towel holders on the floor, which are now in pieces. I reach down to pick one up while Terry howls with laughter.

"McCandless! What the hell did you do?" Mr. Woodwood yells from the front of the class. "You think that's funny?" He sets his box down on the front bench.

"I didn't do anything," I reply, holding a piece in my hand. "They just fell."

"I saw you knock them over, McCandless. Get away from there!"

"He never touched them," Terry exclaims. "They fell when you shut the door."

"Go wait outside Mr. Bailey's office," Woodwood barks. "Now!"

"I told you, I never touched them."

"Go!"

I'm waiting in Headmaster Bailey's office when Mr. Woodward arrives with some pieces of a broken towel holder which he hands to Mr. Bailey. "McCandless knocked over the previous class's finished work. It's all destroyed and will have to be redone." His face reddens as he adds, "He thought it was hilarious."

178

Mr. Bailey looms over me. I smell coffee on his breath. "Well, what do you have to say for yourself?"

"I never touched them," I answer. "And I wasn't the one laughing." I look up at his shiny, bald head. I never realized until now just how big his ears are.

Bailey and Mr. Woodward give each other a knowing glance. "That's not true," Mr. Woodward insists. "I saw him do it."

"You know what's coming now," Mr. Bailey says. "Give me your hand." He grabs one of his favorite canes from his umbrella stand and gives me three good whacks on each palm. After a speech condemning my "reckless vandalism," he adds a week's detention.

This incident permanently brands me as a hooligan in Mr. Woodward's eyes.

Irish Medicine Man

I've had a boil on top of my right foot now for about a week and it's getting pretty sore when I walk. "Mom, look at this. I've got a boil on my foot," I say, yanking my sock off, which is stuck to the sore.

"How long you had that?" she asks, eying the festering mess. "It looks bad. You need to soak your foot. I'll get some hot water."

Bunjy barges in from the kitchen. "What looks bad?"

"Have a look at that boil on his foot. It's infected. You need to take him to see Dr. Milligan to get it lanced."

Bunjy takes a look. "Och, it's just a wee boil. I can take care of that. He needs a bread poultice."

"What do you mean, a bloody bread poultice?" Mom says, walking in with a bowl of hot water. "He needs to see the doctor."

"He don't need no doctor," Bunjy insists. "Let him soak his foot in the hot water and I'll make the poultice. It's an old Irish remedy."

While I'm soaking my foot, he boils some milk and adds slices of white bread to soak it up. I dry my foot and Bunjy tries to drain the boil by squeezing it with his thumbs. The pain is excruciating.

"We need to get that root out," he says having another go. After a few more unsuccessful attempts, Bunjy slaps the warm bread and milk paste onto my seeping wound. "Joyce, cut me up a piece of that old bedsheet." He uses this to bandage my foot.

"Now keep that on," he warns.

"Are you sure about that poultice?" Mom asks.

"He'll be fine. It'll draw the poison out. We'll check it tomorrow."

I hobble to bed, wishing I had never mentioned the boil. After a few days I'm on my fourth poultice application. "It looks like the hole in my foot is getting bigger," I remark.

"It has to get worse before it gets better," Bunjy insists, squeezing hard on my throbbing, bread-encrusted wound. "That root's got to come out."

I sit quietly, wondering how many limbs have been lost to a full course of Irish bread- poultice treatments.

It's time to get changed for a double period of PE at school and I stand outside the teacher's office because my foot is too sore to play soccer. "McCandless, what are you waiting for? Get in the locker room and get changed!" the hulking Mr. Palmer barks.

"I'm not doing PE today," I announce. "I've got a sore foot."

"I can't do it either; I have a cold," another boy declares with a snuffle. Two others complain about stomach flu. Eight of the 20 boys excuse themselves from class.

"What is going on?" Mr. Palmer protests. "It's a beautiful day out there." He moves his large, athletic frame in among us, passing a soccer ball between his huge hands. "PE is for your benefit! It's supposed to be fun, and you pansies don't want to join in."

He bounces the ball and catches it easily with one hand, grabs the whistle hanging around his neck, and blows it like a referee calling a foul. "Okay, thanks to these pansies, no one is doing PE today. You boys who've already changed, get back into your school uniforms."

A chorus of groans erupts from the locker room. "You wankers! Now *we* don't get to play."

"Okay, grab your gym bags and follow me, single file."
Mr. Palmer parades us past the girls' gym class and a handful
of disapproving teachers to a stuffy classroom, which has a
perfect view of the lush, green football pitch outside. "Now,
wouldn't you rather be out there than stuck in here?" he
prods.

The non-sickies deliver another round of abuse on cue.
"Why don't you leave these wankers here and we'll go play
five-a-side?"

"No, no. The class will stick together." Mr. Palmer turns
to the pansies. "So, let's go 'round and see what these
ailments are." After three colds and two stomach aches, it's
my turn. "McCandless, you look pretty healthy to me. What
was it you had, a sore foot?"

"Yes, I have a boil on my foot."

"Did you say boil? Boil? Nobody gets boils on their
feet!" He turns and walks back to the front of the class,
shaking his head.

"What, you don't believe me?" I call after him.

"In all my years, I've never heard that one."

I get up and walk to the front of the class. "Here, I'll
show you!" I plant my foot on the desk next to him.

"Sit down, McCandless!"

Ignoring him, I remove my shoe and sock, then unwrap
the strip of bed sheet, revealing the slice of bread stuck to my
foot.

"What's that, a foot-long sandwich?" Mr. Palmers
chuckles.

I tear off the bread, exposing the green, oozing hole in
the top of my foot. "Do you believe me now?"

The boy whose desk I'm resting my foot on gasps. "Oh,
nasty. That stinks!"

"McCandless, what the hell have you got on there? That
needs treatment."

"Oh, now you believe me." I slap the slice of bread back on and start to reassemble the dressing.

"No! No! No! Leave that off. Come with me." He leads me to the first aid room, where a horrified nurse cleans and dresses my wound. That evening I have to explain to an indignant Irish medicine man that his services are no longer required.

At least I got to keep my foot.

The Blow Up

Because I'm doing well in science and chemistry, our teacher, Mr. Rock, made me class monitor. I assist him with equipment and materials and help him set up experiments.

Today, Terry, Pete, and I are in class cutting slivers of potassium metal off a half-inch cube and placing them in a 4-inch petri dish with water. The chemical reaction causes the potassium to fizz and zip around in the dish.

"Pass us the jug," Pete says. "We need some more water." The two-gallon water jug is passed to our workbench and Pete tops up his petri dish.

Mr. Rock is in his white lab coat and tie, writing on the chalkboard. He walks with a limp and he's missing a lung because of war injuries. He wheezes and pants a lot, especially when he gets upset. We have nicknamed him Rocky.

I'm taking notes when there is a loud explosion next to Pete, followed by the tinkling of broken glass and dripping water.

I look at Pete, who is soaked. "Are you okay?

"I'm fine!" he mutters, wide-eyed. "Terry chucked the whole cube of potassium in the water jug, the bastard!"

Terry has moved back to his workbench, behind ours, and is looking at me with a big, stupid grin on his face. He has both hands on the bench and is trying to look nonchalant.

"What happened over here?" Rocky pants, making his way to our bench. "Are you okay, Nolan?" He checks Pete for cuts and glass fragments.

184

The door bursts open and Mr. Woodward rushes in from his class next door. "What was that explosion? Is everyone okay?"

"Some fool put the whole potassium sample in the glass beaker," Rocky wheezes.

Mr. Woodward eyes me suspiciously, then sends the rest of the class, including Terry, out to the schoolyard. "Was McCandless at the bench when this happened?" he asks. "He has a history of destructive behavior."

Rocky glares at me. "You idiot!" he gasps. "Somebody could have been seriously hurt."

"I didn't do it. I was taking notes," I insist, showing him my soggy notebook.

"Report to Mr. Bailey's office!" he orders.

"He didn't do anything," Pete protests.

"Don't make excuses for this clown," Mr. Woodward snaps, grabbing my arm.

As he escorts me past Terry and the rest of class to Mr. Bailey's office, I can't help but wonder if things would be much worse if I really were the bad bastard they think I am.

Impossible

It's the following week and science class has just ended, leaving Pete and me, as monitors, to break down the equipment. The class was working on pressure measurements using manometers. There are two glass U-tubes set up, one with water and one with mercury. Students have been blowing into the U-tubes through rubber hoses and measuring the pressure. Pete and I decide to try blowing again on the mercury tube.

My mates Colin and Mick poke their heads in the door. "Whatcha doing? Let's go get lunch." Colin is short and stocky, with yellow hair. He's the only 14-year-old I know with a hairy chest and long, bushy sideburns. Mick is slim and about 4 inches taller than Colin. His long, dark hair is parted down the middle, accentuating his high forehead.

"We're trying to hold one atmosphere of pressure with our lungs," I answer. "I should be getting 14.7 psi on this mercury tube; it's not easy."

"Cool! Can I try?" Colin asks.

"Of course, but be quick. You shouldn't be in here." I hand him the rubber hose attached to the mercury tube.

"I bet I can do better than you," he brags. He sucks in a huge breath and braces himself.

"Blow as hard as you like," I challenge. "That thing will measure up to 30 psi."

He forces a blast of air into the U-tube, and mercury explodes out the open end, showering the bench and floor with little rolling globules of the toxic, liquid metal.

"Oh, shit!" Colin snickers, dropping the hose. "Let's go, Mick!"

"You should have known better than to let him try. He inflates hot water bottles for fun!" Mick chortles, and races out the door behind Colin.

Pete and I frantically try to scoop the mercury off the edge of the bench into our hands and pour it back into the half-inch U-tube, but without much success. We have more luck pushing it onto sheets of notebook paper, but there is still a big mess.

Rocky appears out of the storeroom. "You two still here?"

"We've had a bit of a spill," I explain. "We're trying to clean it up."

He limps over to investigate and sees the empty tube and the mercury on the bench and the floor. "How did you manage to spill that? Did you tip the manometer over?"

"No, we just blew on it hard and it came out the other end," I reply.

"Don't lie to me!" Rocky huffs. "That's impossible."

Pete and I look at each other. Colin didn't seem to know it was impossible. We don't want to turn Colin in and we know we'll never convince Rocky of the truth.

"Nolan, go get me the vacuum. You boys can think about what you've done in detention for a week!"

After this second incident, Mr. Rock never again let me touch the materials or the equipment in chemistry class or participate in any of the workshop experiments.

Fork You

It's Saturday afternoon and I'm in the house getting ready for my paper round. The kids are running in and out of the kitchen, and Mom is washing diapers, pushing them through the manual ringer and hanging them on the clothesline in the back yard.

"Get me some pegs and bring 'em out," she calls, carrying an armful of damp diapers into the yard. I grab a handful of wooden pegs and bring them out to her. Her back is turned, and her long, straight, dark hair is tied in a ponytail and swaying gently.

"Keep an eye out for your dad while we're out here," Mom warns. "He went to work early this morning but he didn't take his bike. I'm guessing he's at the pub."

We're on our third load of diapers and the clothesline is almost full when I glance through the fence and see Bunjy's telltale swagger. "Hey, Mom, Bunjy's coming."

"Okay, you kids go play over the marl hole!" Mom hangs the last few nappies and heads back into the kitchen. I have an awful feeling in the pit of my stomach that Mom is preparing for a showdown.

Bunjy barges in past her and rushes into the bathroom. He takes a long, loud, beer piss with the door open. "Joyce, make me a bacon sandwich!" he orders. "I've had nothing since early."

"Why didn't you get something at the pub?" she snips. "You told me you were coming right home. I've been waiting for the money to pay Willis so we can get groceries. We don't have bacon. We don't even have dinner!" she chaffs, making her way to the front room.

"I've got money for you," he barks, following her. He throws a fiver on the table. "Now, make me a sandwich!"

"Make your own bloody sandwich!" Mom screeches. Bunjy lunges at her and I run in between them.

"What are *you* gonna do?" Bunjy prods, grabbing me by the shoulders, his eyes narrowing.

"He ain't scared of you," Mom taunts. "He's getting bigger by the day! He will beat you soon enough!"

"There you go again, turning these kids against me!" Bunjy snarls through clenched teeth.

I grab his arms, expecting him to start swinging punches. My sisters Susan, Sheelagh, and Jean are peering through the middle door, crying and shouting, "Stop it! Stop it!"

"Calm down. You're upsetting the kids," I urge.

But my mom screams like a banshee, lunges over my right shoulder, and rams a dining fork deep into Bunjy's mustache. "There, you bastard!"

Bunjy shoves me away and I step back in disbelief. Mom is still screaming abuse. He turns to me with the fork sticking out of his face, then calmly walks over to the oval mirror hanging above the fireplace. I push Mom behind me, expecting the worst. He yanks the fork out and, to my relief, places it on the mantel. He folds back his top lip and examines the holes in his lip and gums, then spits blood into the fire.

He looks me right in the eye. "See what I'm up against?" Then he walks out the back door.

"Mom, what was you doing? You could have put his eye out!"

"I was *going* for his bloody eye, the drunken Irish bastard!"

189

I back away from her, realizing that she is as crazy as he is. If she were a few inches taller, Bunjy would have a fork buried in his eye.

My older brother's words echo in my mind. "It ain't just him. They're as bad as one another."

"You can't be doing that, Mom. He could have gone crazy and wrecked the house. I don't think I can stop him yet."

Mom's ranting is just background noise to the nightmare scenarios running through my head. Where did Bunjy go? The pubs are closed for the afternoon. Will I be able to protect her when he comes back?

I put my newspaper bag back in the bogey hole. We don't have a phone to call the news agent and tell him I won't be delivering papers this afternoon. It's just as well, since I couldn't explain the situation to him anyway. It's going to be a long day.

Just Plain Weird

Smithy and I are playing football at Jubilee Park after school when I notice Anthony Wilson running by with two of his buddies. Anthony is tall and skinny and has small, deformed hands hanging off his shoulders because of prenatal exposure to thalidomide. He is a couple of years older than I am and goes to a special school.

"Are you Tony McCandless?" Anthony asks, circling around and approaching me. "I hear you can fight."

"Where'd you hear that?" I ask, intrigued.

"Never mind. I want to fight you," Anthony challenges, stretching his legs and trying to look menacing.

"What?" I laugh. "You're kidding, right?"

"What's so funny?"

"Well, you've got no arms."

"He don't need arms to fight you," one of his buddies chimes in.

"Why? Are you gonna help him?" I ask his mates, who appear to have normal limbs.

"Two and half against two seems about right," Smithy says, moving next to me. "We can manage that."

"No," Anthony says. "Just me and you. I'm trained in French kickboxing."

He begins to hop around like Foghorn Leghorn on a frying pan. His mates step out of the way and he moves around me, kicking one leg in the air and then the other.

"Just grab him and knock him out, Tone," Smithy suggests, further intensifying the awkwardness of the moment.

"Back up, Smithy. Let's see what he's got," I say, readily awaiting Anthony's next move.

He tries to kick me in the head and the chest, but I easily block these. Then he spins around and attempts to kick me in the knees, but instead he catches me on the shin.

"If you do that again, I'm going to have to hurt you," I warn.

At that he drops on the ground, puts his legs on either side of mine, and tries to trip me. I reach down and pick him up by his belt. He is looking frustrated and begins to thrash wildly with his legs. I step toward him, grab him with both arms, and drop with him to the ground.

Not wanting to punch him, I decide my best option is to sit on him, a technique I have not previously used in a fight. I plop onto his chest, facing his legs. He is thrashing around like a fish out of water. His friends are painfully aware that I could be facing the other way and pounding Anthony's head. Things are not turning out as they planned.

"Let me up! Let me fight!" Anthony screams hysterically, trying to knee me in the face. *This is getting weirder by the moment.* I decide to sit where I am and let him wear himself out. He is screaming, crying, and trying to bite my arse, but I don't want to be accused again of beating up a handicapped person.

"Take him home," I say standing up. "He's done."

Anthony struggles to his feet, still ranting. He has tears in his eyes and is dripping with sweat.

"Next time I'll get you!" he yells as his friends lead him away.

Smithy picks up the football and we head home. "That was weird," he says, with his cheeky smile.

Prospects

I'm fifteen and the local businesses are contacting our school looking for kids who are good in math and science and interested in doing a trade apprenticeship. My parents expect me to go to work, so I'm considering a trainee electrician's job.

It's school open house day and my mom has come. Headmistress Jackson asks to see us in her office. "Mrs. McCandless, Tony really needs to stay in school and continue his education. He has the skills to go to college and he should do so." Mom doesn't say much because she knows Bunjy would never allow it.

That evening at dinner Bunjy says," I hear your teacher wants you to stay in school. But you're going to work. We need your pay. I've asked at the foundry; you can come and work with me."

"If I'm going to work, I'm going to be an electrician, not a foundry laborer."

Bunjy glares at me. "You'll come with me. You'll earn four times what you would as a trainee electrician."

"I'm not starting in a foundry. I'll be a laborer all my life. If I'm not allowed to go to college, I at least want to learn a trade."

"Fine! You're not going to have much pocket money after paying your board," Bunjy growls, picking up his pork chop. "And there's no shame in foundry work."

Terry's Gift

It's Saturday evening and there's a knock on the kitchen door. It's my mate Terry on his bike. "You got a minute?" He waves me around to the side of the house, reaches into his jeans pocket, and hands me around ten pounds in rumpled notes and coins.

"What's this? Where'd you get it?" I'm looking at what would be six weeks' pay for me delivering papers.

"I need you to hang on to this for me and I'll get it from you later at the disco."

"Okay, fine, but where'd you get it?" I insist.

"You know I work on the cash register at the news agent's on Saturdays. Well, as the day goes by, not all the money makes its way into the till." He grins. "Anyway, I can't take the risk of my old man finding it, the Victorian bastard. He'd have me locked up."

"That's a lot of money. I'm surprised they don't notice."

"Not yet. It gets crazy busy on Saturdays; that's why they hired me. Anyway, keep a couple of quid for yourself. I've got to get back. My old man will be looking for me," he says, speeding off.

Halfway There

I have been selected for a trainee electrician position at Sid Davis Electrical Contracting in West Bromwich. If I pass the medical exam, I can start work next Monday. I'm at a clinic and have just completed the vision and hearing tests, which took a lot longer than I expected. The doctor is a skinny, middle-aged man in a white coat, wearing round, wire-rimmed glasses resting on a nose that looks like a melted crow's beak.

"Sit down, let's go through the results," he says, looking serious. "First of all, the hearing test. You've already lost the higher ranges in both ears, especially the left ear."

He shuffles the papers and looks at some more results. "Regarding your eye test, the good news is, your colors are perfect." He smiles tentatively. "Electricians need to be able to differentiate colors."

"What's the bad news?"

"You've got cataracts in both eyes. The one in the right eye is advanced." He looks intently at me. "Fifteen years old is very young to have advanced cataracts and hearing loss. Can you remember any traumas to your head as a child?"

A bitter smile twitches across my face. *Yes, I can recall plenty, but I'm not about to discuss them with you.*

"It's not funny, young man. In fact, it's quite serious. At this rate, you'll be blind by the time you're thirty. I'm surprised your parents haven't taken you to see anyone about this."

I take a slow, deep breath. "Does this mean I've failed the exam?"

"No. You passed the exam. You're not color-blind. Right now, you can see and hear well enough. But, Mr. McCandless, your parents need to get you to a specialist and get this dealt with."

He signs the paperwork, shaking his head. "I'll send you home with a copy of my report, and I'll call Mr. Davis to let him know you passed."

The two bus rides home give me plenty of time to think. I look at the report, then fold it and slip it into my jeans pocket. I can't mention the doctor's question about head trauma to my parents unless I want to incite further head trauma.

The heavy rain on the bus window blurs my view of the smoke stacks spewing their dark plumes that fold into the rain clouds. Sitting alone at the back of the bus, the eventuality of losing my life as I know it by age 30 begins to sink in. I'm already halfway there. I have a lot to sort out in a short amount of time.

The rumbling of the bus seems to be shaking things loose inside me. Fueled by a renewed resentment toward Bunjy, a part of me is letting go, letting go of the life I thought I would have, as well as any sense of self-preservation. If I can't see, I might as well be dead. I can't imagine myself bumbling around with a white cane.

Everything I try to build gets unraveled, and the threads always lead back to Bunjy.

Brown Halos

It's Saturday night and I'm out with Mick and Terry, approaching a liquor warehouse near Mick's house. "Let's go to my house and listen to records," Mick proposes, taking a drag of his cigarette. "My sister's got the new Beatles album, "Abbey Road." We could hit the beer warehouse on the way, and I'll get the drinks."

"What? Are you treating?" I ask, surprised.

"No way! I'm going in the back door," Mick explains.

"I've got enough going on," I counter. "I don't need any part of that."

"Well, at least keep an eye out for us," Mick insists. He and Terry slip around the back of the warehouse.

I stand on the sidewalk with my hands in my pockets. Heavy clouds trap the ash from the foundries and the coal-fire smoke from nearby houses. The air feels thick and burns my eyes as I look up at the brown halos that hang on every streetlight.

Ten minutes later, Mick and Terry emerge with big, clear plastic bags loaded with small bottles of Babycham, cider, and Cherry Bee. "We couldn't find any beer, but these'll do," Terry announces.

"You look pretty obvious with your swag bags over your shoulders," I remark, looking around. "You really don't think anybody's going to notice?"

"You worry too much," Mick chides. "My house is only two streets over. We'll keep away from the streetlights."

Nervously, I follow them as they carry the booty to Mick's house, wondering where all this is leading and wishing I had just gone home.

The Apprentice

I'm fifteen and a half now, and a trainee electrician working at the new Telephone House in Birmingham. I have to take three buses to get there. The job site is huge and bustling with all types of tradesmen, including around ten electricians and another eight of us apprentices. I'm lucky: my electrician, Ray, is patient and easy to work with. He is brawny, with a budding beer belly, thinning black hair, and long sideburns.

On my first day, I meet another trainee called Cedric, a slight, angelic-looking kid with blond ringlet curls and quiet, blue eyes. He looks more like a choirboy than a tradesman. Unfortunately, he is assigned to Bob, a strapping, loud-mouthed bull of a Brummy.

Electrician trainees are generally treated badly, but Bob is notorious for being ruthless with his apprentices. "Fuck me, me drill bit's broke!" Bob roars, grabbing Cedric by the collar and shaking him. "Ponce, fetch me another!"

"Ray, why is Bob such a bastard with Cedric?" I ask, watching the spectacle. "He's just a harmless kid who's trying to learn."

"What you've got to understand, Tony, is that it's always been this way." Ray explains. "We went through it and we hand it down. It's just the way it is. I don't agree with it, but don't interfere."

Over the weeks, I'm astounded at how Cedric takes his perpetual hazing in silence.

"Bob's a right bastard to you, isn't he?" I ask as we bring in a load of conduit. "Why don't you just tell him to fuck off?"

"I can't. He'd send me back to the office and I could lose my job. I'm going to be an electrician, in spite of Bob."

"I don't know how you put up with him. What's the worst thing he's done to you so far?"

"Well, last week Bob and the others hung me out the 12th-floor window on some wire."

"What did you do?"

"Nothing. After a while they just pulled me back in. I think they want me to crack so they can send me back to the shop. It's not going to happen," Cedric says coolly.

I think to myself, *For a little guy, he's got some big balls.*

It's lunchtime and I'm walking through the basement looking for Ray when I see Cedric hanging upside-down, tied to a 6-foot cable drum. "Come on, let him down," I say, walking toward him. I'm surprised to see that Ray is among the tormentors, sitting on a pile of sand, eating his lunch.

"Tony, stay out of this," Ray warns. "It will only get worse."

"Hey, rookie! Get away from him!" another electrician barks, and they all start throwing sand at Cedric. They roar with laughter when a handful hits him in the face. He spits out a mouthful of sand and quietly looks up at me. They only stop when I walk away.

"Bastards!" I say as I walk out.

After lunch, Ray tells me to report to the foreman. He's tall with a thinning crew cut and a pot belly that hangs over his belt. "See that load of tubes, kid? I want them in the storeroom on the tenth floor," the foreman says, pointing to a pallet of fluorescent lights. "Come see me when you're done."

The packs of tubes are one foot by one foot by eight feet long and very fragile. There are around 100 packs. I spend an hour loading up the freight elevator and moving the tubes to their destination.

When I'm finished, I go back downstairs and bump into the foreman. "What about them tubes?"

"I'm done."

He puts his hand on his hip. "What do you mean you're done?"

"I used the freight elevator."

"Who told you you could use the freight elevator?" he says, looking annoyed. "Go bring them all back down using the stairs, and then take them back up again," he commands.

"Bollocks! What's the point? I did what you asked!" I walk away. *Please send me back to the office. I would love to explain this to the owner.* Then it occurs to me this is probably payback for trying to help Cedric when he was tied to the drum.

Each morning, two apprentices are assigned to go to the cafeteria to get breakfast sandwiches for the crew. This morning Cedric and I have to do it. Around nine o'clock we collect the sandwich orders and rush over to the cafeteria to get back in time to make cups of tea and have everything ready for our ten o'clock break.

We arrive with the box of hot breakfast sandwiches and I go into the kitchen and start making tea, then head to the break room to help Cedric lay out the sandwiches. As I walk in, I'm blinded by his snow-white, bare arse. He is facing away from me with his pants pulled down.

"What the fuck!" I shout. I walk around him, thinking I have caught him jacking off, but to my horror, he has a bacon sandwich wrapped around his dick and he is rubbing it back and forth.

"What the hell are you doing?" I exclaim, remembering that I had ordered a bacon sandwich.

Cedric is unfazed. "I'm nobbing Bob's sandwich. I do this every chance I get," he says, grinning devilishly. "Then I get to watch the bastard eat it."

Cedric expertly rewraps the sandwich and places it next to Bob's mug of tea. He puts his own sandwich directly across from Bob's. The crew shows up, and we all sit down to eat.

After a few minutes, Bob looks up at Cedric. "What are you looking at, you queer little fucker?" he roars and he takes another bite of his sandwich. "Get that stupid grin off your face!" But Cedric never takes his eyes off him and sips his mug of tea quietly.

The crew has left and we are cleaning up. "Fuck me, Cedric, if ever Bob found out, you know he'd kill you."

"Don't worry. He won't figure it out. He ain't smart enough." Smirking, Cedric walks out, refreshed and ready for work.

It all makes sense to me now. Quiet little Cedric doesn't get angry; he gets even. As I wash the tea mugs, I can't help but wonder what other mischief the real Cedric is up to.

Leaving So Soon?

It's Saturday afternoon and Terry, Mick, and I are heading home from the swimming baths. We walk past a nice-looking bungalow with leaded windows and a wrought iron fence. "I'm going in here," Terry says, gesturing toward the house. "I've been watching this place for a while."

"It looks like it's empty. I'm in," Mick says eagerly.

"Not again, are you kidding me?" I grimace. "I'll be over at the park." I walk away.

I watch people fishing from the bank and others in rented rowboats for a while, and then Mick and Terry catch up with me. Terry is wearing a nice gold-colored watch. "Like my new watch?" he gloats. "I got some cash, too."

I shake my head. "You're crazy! How are you going to explain that watch to your old man?"

"Don't worry, he won't see it," Terry says. "Anyway, we better get out of here."

We split off at the railway crossing and I walk home by myself, thinking that Mick and Terry's antics are getting out of hand and resolving to spend more time with my girlfriend.

A few weeks later I'm in the Lee Brook Road Cafe with my girlfriend, Christine, playing "Question" by the Moody Blues on the jukebox and eating my usual egg and chips. Christine has smiling eyes and long, dark hair framing her perpetually cheerful face.

Terry bursts in with some of his friends from the Prince's End gang. He is wearing his new watch and gives me a handful of coins for the jukebox. "Load it up, Tone, we've been busy," he brags.

"I don't want to hear about it." I nod toward Christine, who is picking out songs. "How long have you been running with them? You know that one's trouble." I point to an older, red-haired lad with freckles.

"Well, I don't see much of you these days. You're always hanging with the girlfriend." Terry orders himself a bacon and egg sandwich with a cup of tea and sits down with his new buddies.

Christine and I stand at the jukebox while Terry and his mates throw money on the table and divvy it up. A middle-aged man in work clothes, sitting alone by the window, is watching intently. I walk over to him and he slips a notebook under his newspaper, which is open to a crossword puzzle.

"Can I have a look at your paper?" I ask. "I want to check the movie times."

"Sorry, mate. I'm halfway through my crossword. You can have it when I'm finished."

"Okay." I look him in the eye. "I haven't seen you in here before. Do you work at the steel mill down the street?"

"Yeah. I just stopped in for a cuppa."

"What do you do at the mill?"

"Why do you ask?" he eyes me suspiciously, and I reciprocate.

"No reason," I reply. "I just know a few electricians down there, that's all."

I walk over to Terry and squeeze in next to him on the bench.

"Terry, don't be too obvious, but take a look at that bloke over there." I nod toward the window. "I think he's a copper. He's been taking notes and pretending to do his crossword."

Terry glances over at him. "You're crazy, Tone. He's in work clothes. He's just having a cup of tea," he insists.

Terry gestures to his friends. "Anyway, you know Red, but I brought the rest of the gang here so you could meet them."

"Not right now, I've got a bus to catch." I grab Christine by the arm and lead her toward the door.

"Wait, we haven't heard our song yet," she protests.

"Come on, we'll be late for the movie," I insist.

The man with the newspaper watches my every move. "Leaving so soon? Still want the newspaper?" he fishes as we walk past him and out the door.

Stiletto

It's Saturday afternoon and I'm sitting on the wall in front of our house, waiting for my mate, Pete. The sun is warming my back when I hear a man and woman arguing, their angry banter getting louder. I see a young couple taking the short cut across the marl hole.

"Why were you talking to that poser that rides the Lambretta?" the bloke yells at the girl. "You showed me up in front of my mates!"

"I know him from work, you idiot!" she snaps. "Don't be so bloody jealous!" She turns on her stiletto heels to face him. "If you sat with me instead of drinking at the bar with your mates, maybe he wouldn't have come over."

"If you weren't sitting there with your miniskirt pulled up like a trollop—"

"Fuck you!" She swings her purse at him, but he catches it, slaps her face hard, and knocks her down.

"You bastard!" she yells, struggling to get up.

I run over. "Hey! Less of that! Don't be hitting her." I push him back and reach down to help the girl up.

The young man swings at me. "Stay out of it, you wanker!" I duck and throw a punch that knocks him down and makes his nose bleed. I grab him by the collar to hit him again and feel two sharp blows on the top of my head.

"Leave him alone, you bastard!" the girl screeches. "It's nothing to do with you!" I turn around to see the girl swinging at me again with her stiletto heel in her hand.

I catch her arm and push her away. "Are you crazy? He hit you. He knocked you down!"

"I didn't ask for your help." she screams. "Stay out of it!" She puts her shoe back on and tenderly dabs her boyfriend's bloody nose with her handkerchief.

I shake my head. "You two are welcome to each other!"

I turn to go home, and the belligerent couple follow me, arm in arm. "We're not done, you and me," the young man calls after me.

"I live right here," I say, pointing to my house.

I'm rubbing the rapidly swelling lumps on my head when I notice Bunjy leaning on the wall with a mug of tea in his hand. He's been quietly watching the skirmish. "That'll teach you to mind your own business," he says smugly, and walks back into the house.

Where Are the Clowns?

It's been months now since I've had anything to do with Terry and his crew. I've been focusing on my apprenticeship and spending time with my girlfriend, Christine. Mom's pleased with my progress and the extra money I'm bringing into the household.

One night, it's dark and raining heavily when I get home from work. Mom is in the kitchen. "Hey, Mom." I hang my wet coat on a chair. "Nasty weather."

She looks at me, worried. "There's been a cop here looking for you."

"Did they say what it's about?"

"No. He left his card, though." She hands it to me. "They want you to go down to the station tonight. What do you think they want?"

"I have no idea. I'll go find out." I put my coat back on and step out into the storm.

I arrive at the police station sopping wet and hand them the business card. A uniformed policeman escorts me to an interview room. "What's this about, officer?"

"Detective Brody will be with you shortly." He leaves and locks the door behind him.

After a while, two men in jackets and ties walk in. "McCandless, isn't it? I'm Detective Tom Brody and I believe you know Detective Greene." They sit down opposite me and drop a thick file on the table.

"Seen any good movies lately?" Detective Greene needles.

Brodie informs me that Terry and his crew have been caught red-handed committing burglary and are locked up in cells here at the police station. "We've been after these clowns for a while. They had quite a run."

He puts on his glasses and opens the file. "We have statements from your friends connecting you to some of their earlier escapades. And a report from Detective Greene here placing you at the Lee Brook Cafe, where your buddies split up the loot."

"When did it become a crime to eat in a cafe with your girlfriend while you're waiting for a bus?" I ask. They ignore my question.

I sit quietly and ponder which of my "friends" mentioned my name and why.

Brody unscrews his fountain pen. "We're gonna go over these charges and get a statement from you."

Because there's no actual proof of my involvement, after the interview I'm allowed to go home and await a court date. Terry and his crew remain in custody.

A few weeks later at the hearing, the judge expresses his outrage at the extent of the crime spree and makes an example of us all. Everyone mentioned in the police report receives a sentence, and I'm given three months at a juvenile detention center. Terry and his gang receive longer sentences, which include a stay at a tough London prison called Wormwood Scrubs.

The Set Up

Before going to the detention center, I spend three weeks at the Brockhill Remand Center. My solid concrete cell is about six feet wide by nine feet deep. A barred window on the back wall straddles a small, wooden desk with an uncomfortable chair and a metal-framed cot with a thin, straw mattress. There is no toilet, only a galvanized metal bucket. I'm grateful not to have a cellmate.

A lot of the inmates on my wing are older than I am, and many of them are not first time residents. Most appear to be well on their way to becoming career criminals, and I can see I'm going to have to learn the ropes fast.

New inmates are tested, and if they don't push back they're ruthlessly victimized. In the first week, I've been in numerous altercations and some of the guards have taken notice of me. Butch, a brawny guard with a crewcut, sees me throw my neighbor, Vinnie, out of my cell. "Oh, we've got a tough guy!" he remarks.

"The bastard was stealing my stuff!" I announce.

Vinnie looks like the quintessential villain with his jagged haircut, five o'clock shadow, and crooked, yellow and brown teeth. "No, I wasn't," Vinnie lies. "I was just returning his book."

"You're both on lockdown for the rest of the day!" Butch barks. He is close enough for me to smell the coffee on his breath. "I'll be watching you, McCandless." He tosses me back into my cell and slams the door. I hear his keys jangle as he locks me in.

I grab my copy of Ian Flemming's *Goldfinger* and flop onto my cot. *Hmmm. Coffee would be nice. But I know I won't be tasting that for a while.*

It's dark out and I hear the clatter and banter of the other inmates making their way to the mess hall for supper, then silence. I go back to my book. James Bond is about to do the nasty with Pussy Galore when I hear someone open my view port. I see a blue eye watching me and smile to myself, thinking, *That can't be Bunjy, can it?* As I turn back to my book the cell light is switched off, leaving me in the dark for the rest of the night.

The next morning, I'm in the metal shop, getting ready to assemble bed frames. I'm standing in line to sign out my tools when I notice a big, blond thug giving me the stink eye. I hope the dumb bastard doesn't make his move here, because Butch is on workshop duty and he's eager for any excuse to throw me in the hole.

I take the tools back to my bench and keep an eye out for Big Blondie. I have to assemble a minimum of three bed frames before lunchtime. After the second bed frame, I raise my hand and ask for a bathroom break.

"Wait a while," the guard says, glancing over at Butch. I see from his shirt that his name is Patrick. He is shorter than Butch and has a dark, manicured mustache. I go back to my work.

A few minutes later Patrick shouts, "McCandless! Bathroom break! Now!" I drop my tools and walk across the shop to the bathroom. He searches me before I go in. As the door closes behind me, I'm met by the blond thug, squaring up to me with fists raised.

"I hear you think you can take me," he grunts.

"Where'd you hear that?"

"From Butch." He moves toward me menacingly.

This wasn't the type of shit I was hoping for.

"Look, you and I are probably gonna get into it at some point." I say. "But right now, we're being set up."

"What do you mean?" he says, frowning.

"I guess any minute now Butch and his sidekick will come rushing in here. If they catch us fighting, they'll beat us around this bathroom and throw us in the hole."

"You think so?"

"I'm pretty sure." I turn on the tap to wash my hands just as the door bursts open and Butch and Patrick come rushing in, truncheons drawn.

"What's going on in here?" they shout with gleeful anticipation.

I look up from washing my hands. "Nothing. I was just chatting with my buddy here." I nod over to Blondie, who has dropped his fists and is trying to look nonchalant.

The guards look at each other for an awkward moment. "You gay bastards!" Butch sulks. They grab us by our shirt collars and throw us out of the bathroom. "Get back to your benches!"

At the end of the shift I'm standing in line to sign in my tools when I feel a tap on my shoulder. It's Big Blondie. "Thanks, Mac. You're all right," he grunts. I nod quietly at him, but I'm thinking, *Butch ain't done with me yet.*

Good Neighbors

A few days later, I'm on my cot reading, locked down for the night. "Oi! Mac! Come to the window," Vinnie calls from next door.

"Bollocks!" I grumble. "I'm reading!"

"I need you to pass something to the guy next to you."

Intrigued, I walk to the barred window. "Grab this!" he shouts. Vinnie has tied something into the leg of his overalls and is swinging it over to me.

"Are you out of your fucking mind? They're going to see you!"

"No, we do it all the time," he insists. "Grab it!" I hear the clanking of keys, and Butch and his buddy Patrick burst into my cell.

"Contraband search!" Butch shouts, whacking me around the shoulders with his truncheon. "We've got you now, McCandless!" They shove me onto the cot and slap me around. "Turn-over search!" They tip me and my bed onto the floor and push me into the corner. I watch as they ransack my cell and find nothing but a Mars bar.

"If you wanted that Mars bar, you could have asked me," I quip. That earns me another dig in the ribs.

They are disappointed that I didn't take Vinnie's bait and are forced to end their folly early. "Get this place put back together!" Butch orders. "Consider yourself on report!" They slam the door shut and I expect to hear them move on to Vinnie's cell, but they don't.

My bruised shoulders and chest move stiffly as I reassemble my cell. No longer in the mood to read, I climb into bed and pull the covers over my head to block out the light my visitors intentionally left on. This place is getting to feel more and more like home.

The Special

I'm on the bus being transferred to the youth detention center, glad to be leaving Brockhill behind. I haven't heard music for three weeks and I'm quietly enjoying the radio station the bus driver is listening to when the Simon and Garfunkel song "El Condor Pasa" comes on.

I interrupt the conversation between the driver and the burly guard. "Could you turn that up?" They both look at me, annoyed.

"What, this?" the guard asks, pointing a meaty finger at the radio. "You like this song?"

"Yes."

He switches off the radio. "That's the last music you'll be hearing for a while. I don't want to hear another word out of you."

I slouch back in my seat, listening to the rumble of the diesel engine. "You should've kept your fat mouth shut," a greasy-haired lad with tattoos growls over my shoulder.

After a long, boring bus ride, I check into the detention center and receive my new uniform. I'm now dressed in a lovely, pinstriped, collarless shirt, oversized blue jeans (not Levis), and heavy, army-issue, black shoes. All this is complemented by my "clowned-out," bushy hair, which has not been cut in months.

After a tour of the facility, we newbies are lined up outside the mess hall. "This is where you'll be getting your three squares," Mr. Adams, a heavy-set, middle-aged guard in a sport coat and tie explains. "Some of you will be assigned to kitchen duty."

I take in the aroma of hot food. "Kitchen duty, I'll volunteer for that!" I announce.

Mr. Adams glares at me. "I'll tell you where you're going to be assigned, Bozo! And put your hand up if you want to speak!" He walks over and grabs me by the hair. "You need a haircut!"

"What, now? I thought we were going in for lunch," I protest, with my belly rumbling.

"What, now, *sir!*" he barks. "McCandless, right?" he says, looking at his roster. "You boys stay at attention here." He marches me down the hall to the barber, knocks on the door, and leads me in.

"Bob, this is McCandless. He needs the special." Mr. Adams grins. "I'll pick him up later." He closes the door behind him.

The balding barber shoves me into his chair. "Hey, that's a nice head of curls you've got there, boy," He wraps the cape around my neck. "What'll it be?" he bellows.

"Well, knock it down about an inch on the top, short over the ears, and leave it longer in the back," I say, looking at my reflection in the full-sized mirror.

"Okay, let's see what I can do." He grins and fires up his electric sheep shearer. He starts at the nape of my neck and mows a 2-inch strip just right of center all the way to my forehead. He continues until one-half of my hair is shaved down to 1/16 of an inch, and he leaves the other half untouched.

"How's that for starters?" He smirks, watching me in the mirror.

"Well, it's a bit shorter than I normally have it," I reply calmly. "Let's see what it looks like when you're done."

"It's lunchtime. I'll have to finish this later." He calls Mr. Adams on his walkie-talkie. "He's ready. Come and get him."

Mr. Adams steps in. "Wow! That's an improvement!" He chuckles and leads me into the hallway. "Now, this is what you're gonna do." He puts his face close to mine. "Lunch is over and you're going to collect all of the dirty dishes and wipe the tables down. Got it?"

"Got it."

"Got it, *sir!*" he snaps. He walks me into the crowded mess hall to a chorus of laughter, wolf whistles, and commentary about my new "demi bozo."

"Right, he's on jankers," Mr. Adams informs the kitchen staff. "Get him a trolley."

I spend the next 20 minutes collecting dishes, death threats, and other abuse from my fellow inmates. The last of them leave as I'm wiping down the tables. Mr. Adams reappears.

"Okay, I'm done, *sir*. Can I get my lunch now?"

"Oh, you missed lunch. You'll have to wait for supper." He leads me back to the other rookies who are completing orientation. I can see by their reaction they hope that Mr. Adams is not taking *them* for a haircut next.

Mr. Adams assigns us to a dorm. There are 6 single beds per side, each with a thin straw mattress. We are instructed on how to make our beds and fold and stack our gear in the small lockers next to the beds. "If I find anyone's bed or locker not ship-shape, the whole room will be on jankers!" Mr. Adams barks. "You don't want to be the guy responsible for that."

I organize my closet, put my toothpaste in my locker, and head to the assembly area to get my work duty assignment, which is metal shop and bed frame assembly.

After supper, we are sent to our dorms for an hour to get settled before lights out. I'm sorting out my regulation sleepwear, wondering who my neighbors are, when an oversized dwarf comes swaggering in from the showers. He's wearing pajamas bottoms rolled up 12 inches on his stubby legs, no shirt, and a towel over his shoulder. He has short, spikey, dark hair, cocoa colored eyes, and a permanent five o'clock shadow. His hairy chest is muscular and looks normal-sized in spite of his short arms, brandishing biker tattoos.

"Hey, Hanksy!" a skinhead shouts from the bed opposite mine. "No jacking off tonight, give us a break!"

"Bollocks! Don't worry about me," Hanksy retorts. "At least I'm not jumping in with that other skinhead bitch in the bed next to yours, like you do."

"Fuck you, Hanksy!"

I'm taken aback by the fact that my neighbor is a foul-mouthed biker dwarf who apparently jacks off all night.

"Hey, nice hairdo!" Hanksy laughs and hops onto his bed.

"You like it?" I reply.

"Don't take it personal. You're not the first." He smiles and swings his feet, which don't reach the floor. "Call me Hanksy. What's your name?"

"Call me Mac."

"How long you in for, Mac?"

"Three months. You?"

"Nine months to go." He sighs. "You got any visitors coming tomorrow?"

"No. My parents don't have a car." I turn toward him, leaning on the shaved side of my head. "How about you?"

"No. My girlfriend dumped me when I got sent here." He shows me a well-worn photo of a normal-sized, good looking, dark-haired biker chick. Then he hands me a photo of an oversized dwarf with long hair and a beard on a Harley. "That's me," he says.

"No kidding?" I act surprised. "Nice ape-hangers."

"Yeah." He smiles proudly. "I had the bike custom-built. Can't wait to get back on it."

The next morning before work duty, I'm back in the barber chair, getting the other half of my head shorn. "Well, how's that?" Bob asks, admiring his work.

The buzz cut exposes my large, rectangular skull, festooned with an assortment of lumps, knots, and scars from years of "fun" at the marl hole. Even I have to admit it's pretty shocking.

"Looks great, Bob. By the way, you can keep the hair." I snigger.

He smacks the back of my head. "Cheeky bastard!"

Later, I'm sitting quietly at lunch in the mess hall, not wanting anyone to know it's my 16th birthday, when Mr. Adams approaches. "Happy birthday, McCandless. Enjoying your big day?" He hands me a couple of envelopes.

"Yes, thanks. I'm looking forward to my party," I say sarcastically. "Will there be cake?"

"Will there be cake, *sir*, smartass!" he snaps. "Report to me after dinner tonight. I have something for you."

That evening, I check in with Mr. Adams and get my birthday treat: two hours in the kitchen scrubbing greasy pans while my dorm mates enjoy some quiet time.

It's almost lights out when I get back. I sit on my bed and open the cards. One is from my mother and one is from my girlfriend. I wonder how Mom is holding up. *Is Leslie or Johnny stepping in for me?*

The lights go out and Hanks starts his nightly session under the covers. When he's done, there are a few minutes of silence. Then he begins to weep.

Beam me up, Scotty. I lie in the dark and vow to myself that this will be the last birthday I ever have in a place like this.

Booby Prize

I've done my time and for nine months now have been back at my old electrician job. It's Friday night and I'm in the poolroom at the Ocker Hill Youth Club. We call it The Can, because it's so small that when we have a disco, we're all packed in like sardines.

I'm wearing new Levis, a crisply ironed, yellow Ben Sherman shirt, and shiny, black brogues. I'm six feet tall now and my dark hair has grown long and curly.

"Eight ball, top left pocket," I call, squaring up for my shot. I spot two familiar faces gazing at me from the opposite end of the table. I haven't seen Madelyn or her friend, Linda, since I attended Great Bridge School. Madelyn is all grown up and more beautiful than ever. I smile as I make my shot.

"Rack 'em up, Terry, I'll break," I announce.

"Wait a minute." Terry and Pete move in on the girls. "What's your name?" Terry smiles, leaning on his pool cue.

"I'm Madelyn and this is my friend, Linda."

"I'm Terry and this is Pete," he says with a hopeful grin. Pete steps in. "Hello, Madelyn. Are you with anyone?"

Madelyn ignores Pete's question and looks over at me. "And who are you?"

"Come on, stop messing around." I smile. "You know me."

The girls look at each other and giggle. "No, we don't."

"You don't know me?" My mood begins to shift.

"No. How could we?" Madelyn replies. "It's our first night here."

"I sat one row over from you two in class for years," I hint, walking over to them.

"No, you didn't." Madelyn smiles, basking in the attention.

"This is a new chat-up tactic," Linda chirps. "Tell us more."

I rattle off the names of six of our classmates from Great Bridge School, but Madelyn and Linda still don't recognize me.

"Who cares?" Terry interjects. "Can I get either of you a Vimto?"

"I'll give you a clue girls," I say. "I was the skip-rope booby prize."

They look at each other blankly. "We're sorry, we still don't know who you are." Madelyn swings her long blond hair and gives me her best Lady Penelope look. "But we'd like to."

I feel myself go cold. "I'm Scruffy McCandless. Now get out!" I bark.

Their mouths drop open in disbelief. Then they grab each other and rush out the door.

"Are you out of your bastard mind?" Terry howls. "What was that all about?"

I toss my pool cue onto the table. "I'll explain it to you on the way to the disco. Let's go."

That was the last time I ever saw Madelyn.

It's Time

I've just been across the marl hole to Willis's for sandwich-makings. I'm walking up the side of the house thinking about the two-hour bus ride to work tomorrow when I hear a familiar ruckus—lots of yelling and kids crying. I see Bunjy's bike propped against the wall. *Here we go again.*

I open the kitchen door to find Bunjy with his hands clamped on my mom's shoulders while she recklessly spews insults at him. "Joyce, just shut up!" He shakes her like a rag doll. "Just shut up!"

Mom sees me in the doorway. "Tony, stop him! Stop him!" she yelps. "He's gone crazy!" Terrified, my sisters watch from the front room, crying.

I charge in, grab my mom, and push her into the front room with my sisters. Enraged, Bunjy swings his huge fist at my head, but I block it. Something snaps in my mind and a blackness comes over me. Everything is in slow-motion now, and I'm overwhelmed by the urge to stop him once and for all.

Bunjy's eyes are bulging and he's snarling abuse at me, but I can't hear the words. From low down, I deliver a right cross which catches him squarely on the jaw. He bounces off the coal place door and hits the floor hard. The force of the punch pulls me back to real time.

Mom is screaming, "That's it, Tony! Kill him! Finish him off! I knew you could do it!" My sisters have stopped crying and are hanging onto Mom's dress, wide-eyed.

Bunjy collects himself on the floor. He staggers up, leans on the door, and rubs his chin. Strangely quiet, he looks over at my mom and sisters, then back at me.

I square up and clench my fists. "Come on, it's time," I shout. "Let's finish this!" I watch him intently, waiting for him to make his next move so I can pound him into the ground. He steadies himself, then without a word walks out the kitchen door and closes it behind him.

"Stay here," I tell my mom and sisters. I walk into the back yard, expecting Bunjy to attack me with the garden fork or shovel. Seeing that he and his bike are gone, I let in a deep breath. Mom is holding onto my sisters, nervously peeking through the open doorway.

"It's okay," I say. "He's gone."

Mom runs out onto the step and throws her arms around my neck. "I always knew you could do it! Things are going to be different around here from now on..."

Her giddy accolades fade into the background as the reality of my existence transforms. I think back to that night when I was five years old and the promise I made to myself. *It's over.*

Epilogue

Although we had arguments and tussles during the years that followed, my father never beat me again. I moved out at age 18 and my brother Johnny took over protecting my mom.

After having ten kids, my parents divorced, then remarried, had three more children, and got divorced for the second and final time.

Years later, my father was checked into a hospital with end-stage alcoholism. After watching most of his wardmates die over the course of a week, he walked out of the hospital in his pajamas. He returned to Northern Ireland and lived with his sister Jean, joined Alcoholics Anonymous, and quit drinking and smoking. For the last 20 years of his life, he helped many suffering alcoholics become and stay sober.

At age 34, I moved to California and married the love of my life. Out of the old environment and behavior patterns, I was able to start anew. I had surgeries to repair my eyesight. I built a career in Silicon Valley and ended up living in Santa Cruz, where each day, I am grateful for the life I have now.